D1295948

MEDIC!

MEDIC!

How I Fought World War II with Morphine, Sulfa, and Iodine Swabs

ROBERT J. FRANKLIN

With a foreword by Flint Whitlock

UNIVERSITY OF NEBRASKA PRESS   LINCOLN & LONDON

Library of Congress Cataloging-in-Publication Data
Franklin, Robert J. (Robert Joseph), 1917–
Medic! : how I fought World War II with morphine, sulfa, and iodine
swabs / Robert J. Franklin ; with a foreword by Flint Whitlock.
p. cm.
Includes bibliographical references and index.
ISBN-13: 978-0-8032-2014-0 (cloth : alk. paper)
ISBN-10: 0-8032-2014-6 (cloth : alk. paper)
1. Franklin, Robert J. (Robert Joseph), 1917– . 2. World War, 1939–
1945—Medical care—United States. 3. Medicine, Military—United
States—History—20th century. 4. United States. Army. Infantry
Regiment, 157th. 5. World War, 1939–1945—Campaigns—Italy.
6. World War, 1939–1945—Campaigns—Western Front. 7. World
War, 1939–1945—Personal narratives, American. 8. United States.
Army—Medical personnel—Biography. I. Title.
D807.U6F73 2006
940.54'7573'092—dc22
2005023236

I dedicate this book to the gallant men of the 157th Infantry Regiment of the 45th Division—particularly to I Company, which, according to First Sergeant Willard Cody, turned over seven times in manpower in the course of two years in combat.

And to my children—Pamela, Charles, and Patricia. Someday they might be interested in what their dad did in the war. Though they were born after the war, the wonder of them kept me sane.

Most gratefully, to my wife Betty, my fiancée during the war, who wrote me a letter every day for two years—and waited, and waited, and waited.

CONTENTS

ILLUSTRATIONS

Map

Figures

Illustrations follow page 66

Almost invariably, the World War II combat veterans I have interviewed have said either "thank God for the medics" or "the medics were the unsung heroes."

That being said, it seems strange that until now very little has been written by, or about, the combat medics of World War II. But with the publication of this remarkable memoir by Robert "Doc Joe" Franklin, a medic who served from 1943 to 1945 with Company I, 157th Infantry Regiment, 45th Infantry Division, this oversight is well on its way to being corrected.

First a word about the 45th Infantry Division, nicknamed the "Thunderbirds" after their southwestern heritage. The division originally was a National Guard outfit comprising primarily men from Colorado, Oklahoma, New Mexico, and Arizona— including thousands of Native Americans—although this regionality was diluted once the war began and enlistees and draftees began to join the unit.

National Guard units were generally disdained as the army's poor stepchildren, their part-time soldiers having to make due with obsolescent equipment, outdated uniforms, and inadequate training schedules and facilities. But after the 45th was federalized and placed on active service in September 1940, then underwent over two years of extensive and intensive training, the Thunderbirds became the equal of any "regular" infantry division.

In the summer of 1943 the 45th was deployed overseas to the Mediterranean Theater of Operations to take part in the invasion of Sicily. So impressed was he with its ability to accomplish its very difficult missions that Lieutenant General George S. Patton Jr., commanding the U.S. Seventh Army during the operation, said that "the 45th Infantry Division is one of the best, if not the best division that the American army has ever produced."

Such praise carried a steep price. The better the Thunderbirds fought, the more often theater and corps commanders sent them into combat. The 45th went on to compile one of the most heralded combat records of any American unit in World War II—and one of the highest casualty rates.

After the month-long Sicily campaign was concluded, the division participated in the invasion of Italy at Salerno and made a monumental defensive stand that earned it considerable plaudits for preventing the Germans from splitting the British and American landing forces and throwing them back into the sea.

After months of slogging up and down the rugged Apennine Mountains on the drive northward and being unable to break through the German defenses around Monte Cassino, one hundred miles south of Rome, the Allies decided to make an end run around the German defenses and land behind enemy lines at Anzio. It was again the 45th that was inserted into the hottest spot on the battlefield and took everything the Germans could throw at it—from suicidal infantry and tank charges to a pummeling by the huge shells from massive guns known as "Anzio Annie" and the "Anzio Express." The Thunderbirds lived a life of unremitting misery at Anzio: rain, water-filled slit trenches, and the ever-present specter of sudden and violent death. If war is indeed hell, the devil had no place more hellish than Anzio.

Even the eventual Allied triumph at Anzio and the capture of Rome on June 4, 1944, did not earn the Thunderbirds a rest, for they were one of the units selected for Operation Anvil-Dragoon—the invasion of southern France in August 1944—the division's fourth amphibious combat assault. From the sunny Riviera, the 45th, along with other units in the Seventh Army, battled its way up the Rhône valley in southeastern France, into the winter nightmare in the Vosges Mountains, through the fortified Maginot and Siegfried Lines, and into Germany itself. Five more months of brutal, unremitting fighting lay ahead, culminating, in April 1945, in the liberation of the Nazi concentration camp at Dachau and the capture of Munich.

The price of victory was paid in blood by the men of the 45th: in 511 days of combat, the division, with an authorized strength of 14,253 men, suffered over 100 percent casualties—4,080 killed, 16,913 wounded, and 3,617 missing in action. Only three other American army divisions (out of a total of ninety-one) suffered more casualties.

Through almost all of this incredible saga lived a medic (and writer) named Robert "Doc Joe" Franklin, who was drafted in 1942 and assigned to the 28th Infantry Division. He was reassigned to the 45th shortly before it left the United States for the Mediterranean in early June 1943.

In *Medic!* Doc Joe's spare, unadorned, and detailed prose tells it like it was—the mud and blood of the battlefield; the innovations in emergency medicine he had to contrive; the crazy and unbelievable-but-true episodes that happen only in combat; the colorful, unforgettable characters; the heartbreak of continually losing his best friends to enemy (and sometimes "friendly") fire; his own efforts to overcome pain and exhaustion to attend to the wounded—both American and German—under fire; the arrogant stupidity of some officers who got their men—and sometimes themselves—killed.

Doc Joe also lavishes praise on those who most deserve it: the individual soldiers he was continually called on to save—ordinary American boys caught up in a war none of them wanted but that they took part in because it was their duty, and who daily risked their lives to accomplish their mission. Within these pages you'll meet larger-than-life figures: Willard Cody, Jackson "Cowboy" Wisecarver, Charles Kroetsching, Guy Pearce, Leon Shapley, Dr. Irving Teitelbaum, and many more brave men whose only memorial is this book. You will shed a tear for them.

I daresay you will find it impossible to finish this book without being emotionally touched; without being staggered by the sheer brutality of combat and almost unendurable battlefield conditions; without being moved by the enormous heroism and devotion to duty of Doc Joe and the soldiers for whom he so lovingly cared. And quite likely you'll say a silent thanks that the United

States has been able to produce men of the quality of those Doc Joe has immortalized in *Medic!*

Very few memoirs from World War II are as compelling, as eloquent in their simplicity, and as honestly written as this one. This is no sanitized Hollywood version of war, and it should come with a PG rating. Although Doc Joe was no war correspondent, this book ranks with the best of Ernie Pyle and Richard Tregaskis and even the great war authors such as Erich-Maria Remarque, Ernest Hemingway, and James Jones.

It is not a stretch to say that *Medic!* will sear its way into your consciousness and earn a place as a classic tale of men at war.

FLINT WHITLOCK
Author of *The Rock of Anzio*

ACKNOWLEDGMENTS

Many thanks to writer Flint Whitlock for his encouragement and help with this book. Thanks also to my editors at the University of Nebraska Press, Jeremy Hall, Beth Ina, and Elizabeth Demers, for their faith in this project, and to Alice Bennett for a superb job of copyediting. And thanks to my granddaughter Luwana Masteller and my daughter-in-law Debra Franklin for doing all the preparation.

MEDIC!

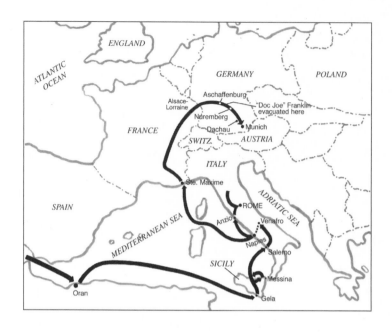

Combat Route of the 45th Infantry Division through Sicily, Italy, France, and Germany, July 1943 to May 1945

Call me "Doc Joe." I'm nobody, and like Emily Dickinson, I don't want to "croak my name the livelong day to an admiring bog."

I was listening to the radio on the Sunday morning in December 1941 when FDR announced the bombing of Pearl Harbor. Bright and early Monday, I was at a navy recruiting office to enlist. They wouldn't take me because the doctor (Joel Pressman, husband to the actress Claudette Colbert) took one look up my sinus-plagued nose and said, "You'll never make it at sea, son." He didn't remember that he had operated on my nose a few years earlier when I was a senior in high school.

So I waited for the army to draft me a few months later. I had been starving while I tried to crack the legitimate theater in New York, so after signing up for the draft in New York in 1940, I had hitchhiked back to California. I finally got a job with the Associated Press as a printer attendant and wire photo apprentice, and though I had then been eating for a year, I weighed only 137 pounds. When, as ordered, I arrived at the draft office in Hollywood to be transported to a downtown Los Angeles staging depot, I was very apprehensive. I had given up my rented room and my job with the Associated Press, gotten rid of all my belongings, and spent my last nickel. I was scared stiff that the doctor giving medical exams before shipping us to Fort MacArthur in San Pedro, California, would not pass me. Thank heavens he did. I don't know what I would have done otherwise. I was twenty-five years old, with no money, no room, and no job.

From Fort MacArthur I and a trainload of others were shipped to Camp Gordon Johnston in Livingston, Louisiana. I was placed in a medical unit with a bunch of National Guard men from Indiantown Gap, Pennsylvania. If you weren't from the Gap, your name was mud. But many men from California were also in this unit, the 28th Division. Before a year was up, the 28th was under the command of General Omar Bradley.

I met Bradley once during maneuvers in Texas. I had been transferred to a signal company, where I worked a switchboard. Having been on duty all night, I was resting in a shallow slit trench and reading a comic book when a kindly voice asked where the regimental headquarters was. I looked up, and there was Bradley looking down on me. When I started to stand he said, "Don't get up, son." I didn't know where the headquarters was, and Bradley and his entourage walked off, gathering sticks for firewood as they went.

After ten months of maneuvers through Louisiana, Texas, and Florida, during which we lost our Camp Gordon Johnston to another division, I heard that a thousand men were being transferred from the 28th to the 45th Division to bring it up to combat strength before sending it overseas. They were being very selective about who they sent to the 45th. Being in division headquarters as a clerk, I went to the first sergeant and asked him to put my name on the list. He did, and I thanked my lucky stars. From what I had seen of the 28th during training, I didn't want to go into combat with it. Most of the men were good, but I had doubts about some of the National Guard boys from the Gap. Some in charge of our training didn't know what combat was and seemed to me to be plain jackasses. The 28th had been in World War I, and the politicians were trying to keep it out of combat in World War II. The division did wind up in England eventually, but it missed the D-Day landing, marched through the Arc de Triomphe after the fall of Paris (without having seen any combat), and was then sent to the nice "safe" Ardennes, where it was surprised by Germans in the Battle of the Bulge and decimated.

For some reason, the 28th Division assumed it was going to the Pacific. Though I had been assigned to a medical unit, I got no medical training. All our training was for infantry fighting—close-order drill, crawling under barbed wire while machine guns fired live rounds over us. (One guy didn't believe it and stood up. He was killed.) I qualified as "marksman" with a Springfield '03 rifle and as "expert" with a tommy gun. While on maneuvers I swung from trees by ropes and went through all kinds of stupid daredevil stunts that we never needed during my two years of combat. I excelled with the bayonet because I had taken fencing in college, and facing steel never bothered me as it did many of the uninitiated. What I learned about first aid, I learned from sitting in an orphanage infirmary as a child and watching the nurse for hours. I had also helped my older brother earn his first-aid merit badge in the Boy Scouts.

No doctor ever talked to us about treating wounds (probably because no one had been in combat). We once got instruction about pressure points and the use of tourniquets to control bleeding, but we were given no training in using the medicine and bandages that would eventually be in our medical pouches.

I was transferred in grade (corporal T-5) to a medical unit with the 45th—still totally unqualified as a medic. I went into combat completely unprepared for the job I was supposed to know. Though I was called a medical corporal technician, I'd been taught nothing about taking care of combat wounds.

After we arrived in North Africa in June 1943, a couple of squads from the 36th Division gave my regiment a demonstration of house-to-house fighting. They fired live machine gun ammo down the middle of the street of a Hollywood-type simulated town while the riflemen raced from house to house, throwing live grenades through the windows and dashing through the front doors to fire rifles at whoever might still be alive. One rifleman stepped too close to the middle of the street and took a machine gun bullet in his leg.

The whole demonstration was immediately stopped. A medic from their unit raced to the wounded man. So did I, and for the first time I saw how to treat a bullet wound. The medic merely poured sulfanilamide powder onto the wound and tied on a small Carlisle bandage. An ambulance took the wounded man away. The demonstration was called off.

I wondered if the war would stop like that when a man was wounded. Ha!

For the next two years I poured sulfa power and bandaged wounds. The wounds were penetrating, perforating, and lacerating: the bullets or shell fragments went in and stayed in, they went in and out, and they sliced through. Broken arms were splinted with bayonets and their scabbards. Broken legs were splinted with rifles. Controlling bleeding was imperative, and tourniquets might be required. Sometimes a wound would bleed a lot, and sometimes there was little or no bleeding—especially wounds from artillery shell fragments. When the shells explode they are white hot, and they cauterize as they cut. (I've seen amputations with no blood whatever.)

You might say I learned my job as a medic through on-the-job training. Sometimes, far away from an aid station, I had to make judgment calls and take risks with my patients. I am *not* a doctor. I think my greatest value was psychological. The men appreciated my being there to take care of them and see that they were evacuated to safety.

Medic! is a true worm's-eye view of my experiences as a combat medic with the 157th Infantry Regiment of the 45th Division during two years of combat through Sicily, Italy, France, and Germany. All names are real. I used detailed notes written during those two years to support my reminiscences.

1

The Invasion Of Sicily

We invaded Sicily just before daybreak on July 10, 1943. "We" means most of our 2,300-ship convoy that had crossed a glassy Atlantic and sailed through the Straits of Gibraltar. The Mediterranean was a beautiful blue, so clear I could see deep into it. Bottlenose dolphins escorted us for hours, zipping in and out of the water. Flying fish zoomed out of the water and soared twenty or thirty feet before nosing back in. It was beautiful sailing all the way until we reached Oran, in North Africa, on June 23, 1943. After the three-week trip, we spent a week of physical conditioning before reembarking for Sicily.

Our ship was the *Francis P. Biddle,* which once carried mail from San Francisco to Hawaii. It was a sturdy ship, as we found after crossing a calm Mediterranean only to have a wild storm toss us around on the night of our landing. Apparently each transport had been fitted with a prow gun. The damn thing fired away frighteningly on the steel deck. I was holding on to my bunk as the storm tossed us, but with the first bang of that deck gun I thought we were under attack. I didn't want to get caught below if we got hit, so I scrambled topside.

I joined a small group of riflemen holding on to a rail around the steel housing that led down to our bunks. The ship pitched like a toy boat in a swirling gutter, and I held on to that rail for dear life. An officer stumbled through the sleet and ordered, "Get below! Make room for the ship's crew to work!" He wasn't one of our officers, however, and we didn't budge. Rather than make a case of it, the officer wisely ignored our insubordination and lurched on past.

Our deck gun was throwing balls of fire shoreward, where they arced gracefully and silently exploded on shore with a dazzling shower that left a dullish red glow in the black night.

Near our housing, Merchant Marine sailors tried to get assault boats over the side. One boat, poised about ten feet over the deck rail, broke loose from a steel cable when the ship lurched into a trough. It slammed into the steel deck with a splintering crash, swung crazily, then flew through the air and smashed against the steel guardrail. The winch operator hoisted the hulk over the side and dropped it into the sea.

A second boat swung out of control off its davit, but the cables held. The sea rocked us hard, and the boat swung outward crazily and missed the rail by inches. On one swing it caught an unwary sailor full in the chest and knocked him overboard. A second sailor working with him dodged a return swing and without hesitation leaped overboard to help his buddy. I slid to the rail but could see nothing but wild, swirling foam.

I didn't yet know the men in my platoon[1]—3rd Platoon, I Company, 3rd Battalion, 157th Infantry, 45th Division—to which I was assigned as a "detached medic." I had volunteered to join the 45th when one thousand men were transferred from the 28th Infantry Division to bring the 45th up to combat strength before going overseas. On that storm-tossed deck, I noticed Private Jackson "Cowboy" Wisecarver for the first time. Somebody started to call him a "son of a . . . ," and before he could finish Cowboy hit the guy so hard he didn't know what happened. During the following year, "Cowboy" was one of the greatest soldiers of my combat experience. He was our company's light machine gunner, and his "kill toll" was uncountable.

A friendly voice asked if he could have his shot of morphine

---

1. A platoon consists of thirty-eight riflemen, one officer, and one medic, for a total of forty men. A company consists of three platoons and a weapons platoon, which has a light mortar, a light .30-caliber machine gun, and a bazooka that is carried by one of the riflemen in each platoon. Each platoon is led by a second lieutenant, and its highest noncommissioned officer is a technical sergeant. The total combat strength of a company is nearly two hundred men.

now in case I wasn't around when he really needed it. It was a good-natured guy named Bove, and I guess he was kidding. In time we became good friends. After the Sicily campaign, he joined a newly organized unit of aggressive fighters called Scouts and Raiders. He was killed about five months later, I believe, in the mountains of Italy near Venafro.

The ship's loudspeaker kept blaring boat team numbers to go ashore, but it was a couple of hours before our number was called. Finally we left the spray-swept steel housing and went down the ladder (stairs) to gather our gear from our bunks. The first boy down vomited all over the steps. Ahead of me, Private Bove slipped and barely grabbed the rail to keep from falling, but he sat down in the worst part of the mess. He swore pretty good and headed for the toilet to clean himself up. I covered my nose and mouth with my forearm and got to my bunk. I joined the platoon at Tech Sergeant Dean's bunk. From there we climbed the same stinking ladder, skittered across the wet, slippery deck, and tried to keep our balance by grabbing at tarp-covered hatches, ropes, or whatever we could reach until we finally ducked into an open hatch that led to the troops' mess hold. From there we crossed to the far end, where we were supposed to climb a ladder to the deck to board our landing craft. However, before ascending, our captain awaited further orders that didn't come.

A half hour passed. We unslung our gear, sat down alongside a steel girder, and waited. Then we were ordered to hug the walls of the hold. A large hatch overhead was removed, and I could see flickering flashes from explosions that lit the night sky. Thick ropes were lowered, and a winch hauled up the floor planks and piled them alongside us at the edge of the mess floor. Cables were then lowered into the hold. Up came a 105-mm field gun. It seemed crazy to send in the artillery before the infantry, but I didn't really care. I pulled my helmet over my face and dozed.

Someone shook me awake. Most of the men were already slinging their gear and moving toward the ladder. On deck, I was surprised to discover the black night had turned to a misty gray morning. The ship still pitched in the angry sea. As last man, I followed our company executive officer, Lieutenant Sturtevant, over the side. I clenched my teeth on my loose helmet strap, clutched the top ropes of the cargo net, and bellied over the rail of the bucking ship. It hit a swell, my feet went out from under me, and I hung in space by my hands. My helmet fell off, jarring my jaw when it hit the end of the strap. I got a foothold on the cargo net and felt my way down. Just as I reached it, the landing craft swung away from the ship, and if I hadn't jerked my legs up, I'd have lost them when it banged back into the ship.

Thirty-eight men from my platoon were huddled in the LCPR (landing craft personnel ramp). I worked my way to the pilot, since the medic was supposed to be last man off. I squatted beneath a 20-mm machine gun mounted on a swivel alongside the pilot. Lieutenant Sturtevant worked his way to the ramp, leaned against it, and waved an okay to the pilot. The LCPR banged into the waves. Cold sea spray swept over us, and salt water trickling from my helmet and combat jacket soaked into my OD wool pants.[2]

Mentioning OD pants reminds me that until the day before the landing, we hadn't been told what we'd be wearing into combat. I thought it would be the garrison fatigues we trained in. The ODs always had to be spick and span and properly pressed and creased. I was wrong. The ODs turned out to be a wise choice. They were warm at night and dried quickly from sweat or rain. Another surprise was that for security reasons we were ordered to remove our "Thunderbird" shoulder patches, which reflected our division's southwestern origin. Then the night before the landing we were ordered to put them back on "to let the enemy know who was coming after him." We were all so inexperienced that we didn't know what the hell was going on. Neither did the brass.

Our craft roared, bucked, and banged into a circle of other landing craft, with a cruiser between us and the distant shore. A high-pitched whine came from the cruiser, and a voice boomed over a loudspeaker, "Reduce speed!" The sound scared me. I thought it would warn the enemy that we were coming. I didn't realize that the sound was going out to sea, not shoreward.

2. OD is olive drab.

Our craft's motor changed from a roar to a purr. We no longer pounded into waves. The cruiser's loudspeaker blared with deliberate slowness: "It is now five o'clock! Continue to circle for five more minutes. A destroyer will lead as close to the beach as it can. It is now 0501! Continue to circle until I give the word 'Go!' Good luck!"

Our craft roared back into the circle of landing craft. Men tightened pack straps, hoisted loads higher, gathered bangalore torpedoes, gripped ammo box handles, and snapped clips of ammo into their M1 rifles. Lieutenant Sturtevant yelled, "Be sure your safeties are on!" Tech Sergeant Dean yelled, "No bayonets! No bayonets in the boat! Leave your life jackets on the beach!"

The men had Mae Wests.[3] I had a flat rubber life belt around my waist, and though I thought about squeezing the air cylinder that would inflate it, I decided to wait until it became necessary.

Time went fast. The cruiser boomed again, "Reduce speed! When you break from your circle, keep an even line! Follow the destroyer! Go!"

We became part of a long, irregular skirmish line as our boat bounded toward the not yet visible shore. All through the night, first waves of landing craft had gone ahead of us. We were the first wave heading for a new beach. In the early morning the dark gray sky turned light. Kneeling men rose to their feet. A kid in the center of the craft vomited in his helmet without first removing the liner. The puke was passed to the side to be thrown overboard, but the stink started a small epidemic of vomiting. A bucket brigade emptied helmets over the side. Being in my position up front, I was spared seasickness. But I did wonder as we bounced toward shore, *"What if the whole thing fails? We're thousands of miles from home. Maybe we ought to go back and practice some more."*

I truly expected to die in my first combat assault. I never expected what happened. Wild as the Mediterranean was, and despite other boats' overturning in the furious waves, our helms-

---

3. Mae West, a popular movie star of the 1920s and 1930s, had a prominent bust (to say the least), and the life jacket was prominent where she was—hence the name.

man made a perfect landing! The ramp crashed down only a few yards from the sandy beach, and we charged ashore. We had hit a "dead" beach—no artillery explosions. No machine guns. No barbed wire. No dead bodies. No opposition!

Down the beach to my right, three Italian soldiers with hands raised high came out from behind some boulders and surrendered to a medic from another boat. Tech Sergeant Dean yelled to us, "Get off the beach! Get inland!"

The beach, about thirty yards deep, was bordered by brush-covered sand dunes. The landing hadn't been so easy for some. In a dune gully, bordered with baby grapevines, I came across seven sopping wet, shivering privates from F Company. Their boat had turned over in the wild surf. Their teeth chattered as they spoke to me: "We couldn't find the rest of our company . . . maybe they drowned . . . you think it's okay to build a fire? We're freezing!"

I had been promoted to corporal back when I was in the 28th Division, so I guess they thought I was an authority. The gully seemed deep enough to be secure from observation. I gave the boy a book of dry matches, poured some spirits of ammonia into a canteen cup of water, and passed it around. I thought it might warm them. Hell, for all I knew about medicine, I might have been poisoning them—but nobody dropped dead.

Someone from the company called me to check on a para-trooper about a hundred yards away. He dangled in his parachute from the branches of an olive tree—the first dead soldier of my experience—a kid of about eighteen from Pennsylvania (according to an ID in his wallet). He looked like a limp marionette, with one arm tangled in his parachute lines as though waving a listless farewell. Five of us cut him down. He wasn't messed up—just a little hole in the base of his skull. Nearby I found the tinny white top of a hand grenade lever. Stamped in the metal were the words "Italia Romano."

Tangled in the trees all around were abandoned parachutes with a crazy-quilt pattern of light and dark green. They were all from the 82nd Airborne, which had jumped off the night before. Parachute silk neckerchiefs became a favorite of former cowboys in the company. On them they looked natural. (The scuttlebutt was that the air corps didn't have enough pilots for transport planes, so it had to use fighter pilots. Some of their navigation was so far off that one planeload taking off from North Africa landed in *Spain*.) There wasn't anything to do for the dead paratrooper except to hail a passing jeep and ask the driver to send someone for the body. Then I went back to my company, which was bivouacked in the brush-covered dunes.

Johnny Matthews, supply sergeant with my platoon, seemed confused about whether he should draw rations for me, the detached medic. First Sergeant Willard Cody said, "He's with your platoon, isn't he? Then draw rations for him!" Cody stayed aloof from the men because he played no favorites—even with his closest buddies from their National Guard days. I was detached from my aid station and sent to I Company, so I wasn't directly under Cody's command; he occasionally did show me his human side—as when he referred to himself as "Mother Cody's little boy Willard." During the next two years of combat, when we sometimes had no commissioned officers, Cody would be up front leading the company. He had great concern for the well-being of his men and never left a wounded man on a battlefield. It was almost impossible to get litter bearers from an aid station; usually they were too frightened to come onto a battlefield. Cody always had riflemen make litters from rifles and combat jackets to carry our wounded. I was never strong enough to carry anyone. He saved my life by not letting me join the company as a rifleman.

Shortly thereafter, we moved toward the city of Comiso, beyond which was our first major objective—Comiso airport. We had no opposition. Sicilian farmers greeted us with olive twigs as we passed through their orchards. Most Sicilian and Italian people we talked to had relatives somewhere in America who were sending them money to help them stay alive during the Great Depression. They didn't seem to have any heart to fight us. One drunk American Indian came in with a long column of captured Italian soldiers. They laughed and waved bottles of vino and shouted, "Viva Americanos! Americani buono! Tedeschi no buono!"

Early on the morning of the second day, we came out of rolling terrain and hit a main highway leading to Comiso. At a fork in the road was a demolished concrete pillbox. By midmorning, uneasiness swept our column. Paratroopers, and whatever other advance units were up ahead, had caught the enemy by surprise. The road was littered with dead Italians and wrecked vehicles. I couldn't tell if there were Germans among them. At first there were only three, sprawled alongside a burned, still smoking Italian scout car. One Italian lay face down in a dust-filled gutter, his left buttock mangled and sopping with blood. The second lay a few feet from him—face upward, mouth open, and lips drawn back in a snarl that showed bad teeth. The third Italian lay sprawled across the legs of the second—his face was a matted, bloody pulp. Almost all the way to Comiso, the road was lined with dead enemies.

It was a hot July morning. Sweat rolled down my cheeks, and I tasted salt in the corners of my mouth. Dust caked my face and hands. I glanced quickly at a knot of dead men tangled with a motorcycle. The flies were feasting.

When we entered, Comiso was a silent, deserted city. Regimental Reconnaissance—Recon—and some tanks had gone through before us, but we were the first infantry to enter. GIs slowly advanced up each side of the street. The city had not been bombed or shelled; there was no damage. Scrawled on a dirty plaster wall was "Viva Duce!"

My platoon stopped at the entrance to the city square. An American tank was parked along its far side, and beyond it was another American tank. Both were buttoned up.

From where I stood, I could look a quarter mile down the sloping road, with GIs lining both sides. No one went into any of the buildings to check them out. Now the men relaxed, leaning against the buildings; they rested their rifles against the walls, tilted back their helmets, and smoked.

A door opened—an Italian soldier carrying a small suitcase stepped into the street. Dozens of safeties clicked, but no one fired. The Italian stood motionless for a few seconds, then walked to the nearest rifleman. Sergeant "Cob" Kennefac waved him down the street. Another door swung open, and another Italian appeared—then another and another, until it seemed the entire Italian army was coming out of those buildings. They all carried suitcases and were waved toward the rear. I don't know who took them from there.

Now the timid civilians came out—women, old men, and children. They laughed and cried with the Italian soldiers, hugged and kissed them, and called good-byes. We weren't shooting anybody, so now the civilians were less afraid. An old man noticed my Red Cross armband. He pointed and cried, "Ah, Croce Rosa!" I became the center of a cluster of gibbering, gesticulating men and women. They felt the texture of my clothes and mumbled, "Buono! Buono!" They peered under my helmet, so I took it off and passed it around; they rolled their eyes as they weighed it in their hands.

GIS soon discovered the secret of popularity—cigarettes. The entire street was filled with smoking, laughing Italians. Halfway down, a small crowd gathered in front of a boarded-up store. There was a lot of milling around and shouting and arm waving. Corporal Moreno of my platoon spoke Spanish and could easily converse with Italians. I asked what was going on, and he answered, "They all got sob stories. Anything they had two of, Mussolini took one. The stuff is locked in that storehouse down there."

What followed looked like a riot scene in Sean O'Casey's *The Plough and the Stars*.[4] Boards were torn off the windows, and some people went in and opened the doors for the crowd. They came out with armfuls of everything—clothing and furniture—and fought over what they had. Lieutenant Sturtevant got the situation in hand by firing one shot into the air. Everybody disappeared like magic.

We stayed in Comiso for less than another hour, then headed out into rolling country. A final sprinkling of Italian soldiers came out to surrender and followed the others down the road. We

4. Sean O'Casey, a successful Irish playwright who wrote *The Plough and the Stars,* was acclaimed in both Ireland and New York during the Depression.

were barely out of Comiso when we had our first experience with German artillery. Three express-train screams cut the air over us, and three explosions followed in the city. If we hadn't left when we did, we'd have had a lot of casualties. But we were lucky, and as more shells whooshed overhead, we jumped into a roadside ditch. A few more rounds exploded, closer, but we had no casualties. The men around me looked nervous. Maybe I did too, but I thought it was exciting.

Sergeant Kennefac, up ahead, called, "On your feet! Get moving!" I left my nice safe ditch and moved forward with the column, now spread out at ten-yard intervals. But I kept my eyes peeled for a ditch to jump into when the next shells came in. Fortunately the Germans stopped shelling.

Near noon we reached a vineyard at the edge of the Comiso airport. We dropped our packs and spread out on the ground in the center of the vineyard. I snuggled down in a dusty furrow between the vines. The sun got damn hot, and I was low on water. Clusters of grapes dangled there for the taking, but they were hard and sour.

Someone called, "Fix bayonets!" Word was passed from man to man, followed by clicks. Machine guns on our left and right shattered the silence, and when Sergeant Dean's voice yelled "Let's go!" GIs erupted from the ground and ran forward hooting and hollering like a bunch of crazy Indians. I ran with them. Carrying less weight, I outran my platoon and had to pull up short to let the yelling riflemen go by. One of the men in my platoon went past me with his pants around his knees. His pack straps had been holding them up, and when he dropped his pack, he also dropped his pants.

The men called him "golden boy," since he was really too old for combat, but he tried. As the men ran past, I had a few seconds to catch his act. He skipped, jumped, and hobbled along with his cartridge belt around his ankles and his pants down to his knees. One hand clutched his rifle to his chest while the other tried to hoist both the ammo belt and his pants. He had a very worried look. I ran forward with the rest of the men.

When I reached the border of the flying field, I hit the ground alongside Sergeant Matthews. He checked his men, and muffled replies came from all directions. No casualties. No one even fired at us. I lay prone next to a solitary olive tree, then stood erect with my head against a low branch for a look-see across the field. There was nothing there except what looked like a small concrete blockhouse. Everyone was still flat on the ground, so I thought I'd better get down too. Just as I started down, a sharp *splat!* cracked into the branch—exactly where my head had been.

The shot came from the blockhouse. First Scout Mike Baca crawled to within a few yards of the small building and blew the door down with a concussion grenade. Through the smoke came three pitiful-looking Italian soldiers. Two had their hands clasped on top of their bare heads and stumbled toward us. The third waved his arms wildly, and his head wobbled as though his neck were rubbery. He ran first one direction and then another, and his legs kept buckling. His two buddies stopped and went back for him. They each gripped him under his armpit with one hand and kept the other in the air as they limped across the field to us.

That was our total opposition right up to the edge of Comiso airport. We dug in behind a four-foot dirt parapet bordering the field. D-Day plus one, and we had captured the Comiso airport.

Until late the next afternoon, German fighter planes coming down from Italy thought they'd be in for a nice, friendly reception. That first afternoon I watched as one of our fighter planes swooped down on three Germans and shot them down as neatly as in a movie.

One of the planes crash-landed less than fifty yards in front of me. As its wheels touched the ground, it hit a hunk of wreckage from a bombing the day before. The pilot flew out of his cockpit, and his parachute opened in a long tail behind him. He came to a sudden stop when his head hit the prop of another wrecked plane. I went to look after him. His brains were exposed. I figured him for dead, but Lieutenant Ralph Barker said, "Check him, Doc. I think he's still alive." I fingered the German's pulse and was surprised to find it was as strong as mine.

I didn't know what to do and was saved when our aid station jeep pulled up with Sternlieb, one of our two doctors. He said there was nothing we could do for the fellow: "Just make him comfortable." The guy was unconscious. How do I make him comfortable?

I cut away the pilot's flying togs to check for wounds and saw two very sturdy legs wearing gabardine shorts. He was a nice-looking fellow. The ID papers in his wallet showed he was twenty-three. There were photos—a family, maybe mother and father, two young girls, a few German coins and several paper marks, postage stamps with Hitler's picture, two paper-wrapped condoms, and a map with a penciled route from northern Italy. The outside of his wallet was marked with the names of various large cities he'd been in. Comiso had yet to be added. His pulse weakened and soon died away. So did he. This was the first man I'd watched die, and I felt sorry for him.

Later that afternoon we were fired on from across the airfield. We had a short but hot and heavy firefight. It turned out we were being attacked by our late-arriving 179th Regiment, who thought we were Germans. Our only casualty was my platoon's BAR[5] man, who twisted his back climbing our dirt parapet to fire back at the 179th. He was in great pain. Morphine didn't do any good. He cried, "My gun wouldn't fire! My gun wouldn't fire!" The next morning a German plane came in to land. As his wheels touched ground, some damn fool across the field started shooting. The German gunned his engine, took off, circled over the opposite field, and dropped a bomb before disappearing in the sky. I was told the bomb hit a command post (CP) of the 179th.

That afternoon I found a nice-looking ivory case about the size of a toothbrush holder. As I reached for it, a training film popped into my mind—"booby traps!" Engineers spent many hours blowing up booby traps planted all around the field. I was also curious about a pile of wooden bullets I found. (I never saw them used until we got into Germany two years later.)

Corporal Moreno and I talked to a wrinkled Sicilian farmer at the edge of the vineyard. I told Moreno to ask him why all the

---

5. BAR means Browning automatic rifle, a carryover from World War I. The ones I saw seemed very unreliable and frequently wouldn't fire. They were carried by some men in the weapons section of the company.

grapes were so small. The farmer answered, "The bombs have frightened them."

Toward evening several of us gathered at a large trash pit. Chaplain Leland Loy was going to hold a service for the dead German pilot, who lay at the edge of the pit. Loy had started to say a few words when the call came, "Saddle up! We're moving out!" Everyone except Loy and I dashed to his outfit. Loy put his foot on the German and said, "May the Lord have mercy on your soul!" He then kicked the German into the pit, mounted a confiscated bicycle, and rode off after the troops. I thought this was strange behavior for a chaplain.

Our next objective was Licodia—a town at the top of a mountain. The people who came down from it to get water at a well looked as if they belonged in the Middle Ages. So did Licodia. A Recon halftrack went into the town and was fired on by snipers. One of the men killed was the brother of one of our squad sergeants, George Hogate. Hogate went up to Licodia and brought his brother down. I was told the Hogates were orphans, so now George was alone. He had an easy smile and a slightly hawkish edge to his face. His shoulders drooped as though from long days slouched in the saddle, and he habitually chewed tobacco. We became good friends, but I wasn't with the company when he got killed.

At the bottom of Licodia's mountain was a small village where the well was. A captain at the well wouldn't let our fellows fill their canteens, saying that the Germans might have poisoned the water. I watched the ragged civilians dip their jugs and drink their fill and didn't see any bodies lying around, so I gathered canteens from my platoon and went to the well. When the captain tried to stop me, I said, "Sir, I've got to have water for men passing out from the heat. Everybody is bumming from me, and I'm all out." I went ahead and filled the canteens and was surprised that the captain didn't know what to do about me. For the first time I realized that a medic could talk back to the brass and get away with it.

The Germans were retreating, and we were chasing them. I stopped to help a GI doubled over with pain. A jeep with two officers came by, and I told them I needed their five-gallon water can. They eyed me suspiciously but reluctantly off-loaded it. I forced the GI to drink several canteen cups of water. When he begged me to stop, I told him to stick his finger down his throat, and he threw up a pile of grape skins. Many of the fellows had been gobbling half-ripe grapes, and I guessed that was his problem. Yet he might just as well have had appendicitis. We were far from our aid station, so I took desperate chances. But what did I know? I made a lucky guess. The two officers were impressed. One asked for my name and unit—I don't know why. They drove off, and I left the boy with the bellyache to recover by the side of the road.

As I hurried to catch my company, a colonel riding a jeep yelled at me, "Goddamnit, soldier, roll down your sleeves and quit straggling!" A few miles past Licodia, another colonel came tearing up in a jeep, skidded to a stop in a cloud of dust, and yelled, "Get these men the hell out of here! The British are going to shell this sector in a few minutes!"

Why they were going to shell it when we already held it is one of the mysteries of war. We had to double-time it back about a thousand yards. Then came the British barrage—and the British. My morale did an inside loop. For some ten days we'd been walking our feet off up and down mountains and along dusty, shell-pocked roads. We knew the Germans had retreated on trucks, but we didn't care—until we saw the British. They were riding on *our trucks!*

We finally did get a ride—all the way south to Gela. From there we rode north again to the Mediterranean coast and captured Palermo with no opposition. Then we headed east along the northern coast. Now we ran into intermittent barrages. We timed the explosions and ran between them with no casualties. Golden Boy refused to run the gauntlet of the barrages, and since I brought up the rear of the platoon, I had to wait for him. Finally I had to leave him to catch the platoon. Golden Boy always showed up later. Maybe he was smarter than we were. Why not wait until the barrage was over?

Near the coastal town of Castel de Tusa, the company pulled

into a deep, narrow ravine just as night fell. My platoon bivouacked in a dry riverbed strewn with mammoth boulders. We had no sooner bedded down than a battery of 105-mms from our 158th Field Artillery support unit set up a few yards behind and alongside us. I don't recall hearing the big guns fire while I boiled a canteen cup of water for coffee early the next morning, but they must have, because a counterbarrage of eighty-eights pounded in on us.[6] With the first explosion I kicked my cup of water into the fire and threw myself between two massive boulders. Incoming shells bounced me up and down so hard I cracked my chin on a rock and was dazed for a minute. Then I called, "Anyone hurt?" Sergeant Dean, nearby, called, "Doc, I'm hit!"

I checked Dean's wound. It didn't seem too bad, so I went to a call some ten yards away. Struble lay there pounding the ground with his fist. Half his foot was hanging by a thin strip of flesh. I'd forgotten my medical pouches and had to return to my "campfire" for them. Sergeant Dean was still lying there. "Be with you soon," I told him. "Struble is hit pretty bad."

By the time I returned to Struble, Lieutenant J. G. Evans and Lieutenant Barker were there looking on. With the K-Bar hunting knife my brother had sent me before I went overseas, I cut away Struble's leggings, his shoe, and his dangling foot. (It was probably the stupidest thing I did in the war, but I was dazed and couldn't see how to bandage it the way it was. If I'd had proper training, I'd have done things differently.) The wound was caked with dirt, and there was no water to wash it. I just poured sulfa powder on the dirt and awkwardly tied on a Carlisle bandage. A couple of the fellows made a litter from rifles and combat jackets and hauled Struble up the mountainside to a dirt road where there happened to be an ambulance.

With the next incoming shell, I threw myself to the ground. When I got up I found I'd slid in a pile of soft shit from my left hip to my knee. Hell! I'd rather have been shot! I used dirt and weeds to wipe myself down.

Lieutenant Barker was alongside me when a fragment from

---

6. Eighty-eights are 88-mm German guns. American soldiers *hated* the eighty-eights.

an exploded shell came screaming straight down—and I mean *screaming!* We froze at stiff attention while that thing came hurtling down. Lying prone would have just given it a bigger target. The shell fragment pounded into the ground only a few feet from us. I let out a deep breath.

I bandaged a few more men—walking wounded who went up to the ambulance. When I got back to take care of Sergeant Dean, he wasn't there. I guess he evacuated himself. I never saw him again.

Evans and Barker had ordered the men to go up the lee slope of the mountain while I cared for our wounded. Now I went up too. When I got to the road, two frustrated ambulance drivers came out of hiding and yelled, "Where's our ambulance?" Apparently the GIs who'd carried Struble—plus the walking wounded—had taken the ambulance.

I climbed halfway up the mountain and came to our company CP with our captain, Barker and Evans, and First Sergeant Willard Cody. They had one pair of binoculars and were scanning the opposite slope, looking for an observer who must have called in the German barrage. Cody said to me, "You're bleeding." There was a little blood on my chin, so I gave him an iodine swab to brush the spot. A few weeks later, a tiny pinhead of steel worked its way out of my chin. I never applied for a Purple Heart, awarded to those injured in action; that would have been an insult to men who were dead or seriously wounded.

Another German barrage hit in the ravine. A call "Medic!" came from below—two and three times. Everybody was looking at me, so what could I do? I clutched my medical pouches and slipped and slid down the mountain into the ravine. I was several hundred feet to the left of the artillery and explosions and ran to cover the distance.

Behind a couple of huge boulders were two litter bearers with a litter. "Come with me!" I ordered and kept going. At first they followed, but when I next looked back, they had disappeared. I was now in the area of the wounded. In a large hole were four artillerymen. "Some of your fellows are wounded," I said. "Come with me." I hadn't even found the wounded men yet, but I guess I wanted company. As one, they got up and came.

There were four wounded men. One had so many holes in him I couldn't believe he was still alive—and conscious. As I worked on him, an eighty-eight screamed in low over our heads and exploded on the ravine wall. My patient looked at me incredulously. I had thrown myself across his body to protect him from further harm. I believed that no one I was working on should get hit again. I wasn't heroic; I did it without thinking. I smiled at my patient and said, "You don't mind if I duck once in a while, do you?" I don't know why, but I just wasn't afraid. You find out about yourself in war.

The artillerymen made litters of rifles and combat jackets and carried my wounded up to the mountain road. The artillery lieutenant came over to me while I worked on my last patient and asked, "Where do you think is a safe place for my men?" A lieutenant asking a corporal?

I told him my company had gone up the lee slope. He thanked me courteously and ordered his men up the mountain. But just as some had started up, he got a fire order and stood exposed on a large boulder yelling, "Fire mission!" His men turned and raced back to their artillery pieces. He yelled a bunch of numbers, and the 105-mms fired. I climbed up to the company CP. They were still trying to spot the observer on the opposite slope. I took a turn with the binoculars and was surprised to see him racing toward what looked like a small cave opening. But the guy was wearing civilian clothes. "There's the son of a bitch!" I grabbed a rifle leaning against the slope behind me. "Okay to fire, Lieutenant?" Barker said yes, and I fired until the empty clip popped up in my face. It felt good to shoot back at someone, though I doubt I hit him.

Barker took out a pencil and notebook and asked me questions. He said, "I'm recommending you for a DSC."[7] I was embarrassed

7. The DSC is the Distinguished Service Cross. The army reduced this to a Silver Star. The DSC, next to the Medal of Honor, was reserved for "killers."

because I didn't know what for. I thought what I did was just in the line of duty.

We left the mountains near Castel de Tusa and continued along the coast highway. At day's end, my platoon bivouacked on a hilltop. Lieutenant J. G. Evans was now leading my platoon. We hadn't had a platoon lieutenant since the landing on Sicily because our lieutenant slipped on a ladder during the wild bouncing of our ship and supposedly broke his leg. I never knew his name. Until the bushwhacking near Castel de Tusa, Tech Sergeant Dean had been leading the platoon.

Now Evans said we'd be here for a couple of days' rest. So the fellows dug slit trenches—narrow foxholes—and bordered them with fruit from an orchard below. Around midnight, however, we were awakened by our platoon runner, Private Henry Fisk. I pointed out Lieutenant Evans's hole, and our two-day rest was over. We were to go to the aid of another company that was in trouble.

2

The Battle Of Bloody Ridge

JULY 28 TO 30, 1943

We dodged intermittent explosions from eighty-eights as we infiltrated the area along a dirt road leading into a dense olive orchard of perhaps ten acres. A hundred yards before we arrived, six riflemen passed us going the other way. All were walking wounded. A sergeant warned us, "Don't bunch up! One shell got all of us!"

We bivouacked in the orchard overnight. In the morning I went to the edge of it, where a huge artillery piece (a 240-mm) was firing. After a few rounds it was towed away—a good thing, because within the hour a German fighter plane swooped overhead looking for it. It dropped a bomb in the orchard and was gone. There were casualties, but none from my company.

Later that morning we crossed a wide, dry riverbed that bordered the orchard and continued to the Mediterranean mountain road some fifty yards away. Engineers, riding bulldozers like cutting ponies, were carving a road down the river embankment where a bridge had been totally demolished and across the rocky riverbed. Though eighty-eight shells were exploding all around them, they seemed to pay no heed and went on with their job. What courage!

The company raced across the riverbed to the far bank and up to a road somewhere between Cefalu and San Stefano—about midway along the north coast of Sicily. Coastal mountains towered above us. Instead of continuing along the coast road, we followed a road inland.

Corporal Moreno paused, sniffed the air, and said, "Germans!" I laughed at him. Up to that time we hadn't met any German infantry. "How do you know?" I asked. "I can smell 'em," Moreno said seriously.

At the next bend a German machine gun hammered down a ravine and onto the road. Before the end of the war, I could smell Germans too. Their diet of sardines and sharp cheese gave them away in warm weather if they weren't careful to cover their feces.

We safely infiltrated each draw and continued until a few officers blocked our way. We couldn't go on until the Germans high on the mountain were knocked off. A major, standing in the middle of the road with legs outspread and an arm stretched upward, shouted, "Go on up, men! There's nothing up there but a couple of machine guns!"

The 1st and 2nd Platoons of I company spread out and started climbing. My platoon scaled a ten-foot embankment, found some level spots, and waited in reserve. I was in our CP with Sergeant Matthews and Sergeant Kennefac and our walkie-talkie operator, Baide Black. (He had white hair, so naturally we called him Blackie.)

It was about noon; the sun beat down on us through scraggy brush. For a while it was quiet, then scattered rifle fire started up all across the slope of the mountain. There were long bursts from German machine guns, and it began to sound like a war. We experienced eight-barrel mortars for the first time. Not knowing German weapons, I thought these were eighty-eights. (What did I know?)

Suddenly, four GI riflemen appeared, dashing down the skyline of a ridge to our right. Exploding mortar shells dogged their heels and chased them all the way to the road. None seemed to be hit.

Blackie's walkie-talkie crackled: "Send up a medic and litters! Our medic is pinned down!" I had no idea of where "up" might be. I slid down to the road, ran to the ridge where the four riflemen had outrun the mortar explosions, climbed the embankment, raced through a natural hollow, and glimpsed, in passing, our Colonel James, a captain, and the unmistakable bulk of the famous war correspondent Quentin Reynolds. He wrote a story about "Bloody Ridge" for a now defunct magazine. I read it and thought it wasn't very accurate. His part about GIs' having to carry water and other supplies up the mountain because mules died doing it was right. The "fighting" part wasn't too accurate, because he was down below while the fighting was up above.

I came to a frightened rifleman crouched behind a bush. "Where's the wounded man?" I asked. He pointed up. "I heard him up there." There was no protective cover. I scrambled up another few yards and came upon three riflemen cringing behind a shelf of rock hardly large enough to cover one. A fourth man lay on open ground. He had been shot in the left eye, and fluid like the white of a raw egg seeped into the hollow of his neck.

Fully conscious, the boy didn't make a sound of complaint as I bandaged his eye. I guess whoever shot him was respecting my armband. He didn't shoot me even though I was fully exposed, and he could have put another shot into my patient but didn't. Private Shulman gave me a hand in dragging the boy down the slope. He wanted to get up and walk, but I knew damn well that the guy who shot him hadn't gone to lunch. He didn't fire at us as we dragged the boy down past the frightened soldier in his bush to a small level terrace that afforded shelter from overhead fire. My patient was going into shock. I sent Shulman down to find the aid station and bring back plasma and litter bearers.

I had left my medical pouches above, and as I started back for them I came across the frightened soldier. He was slumped in the bush and rolled over lifelessly when I tugged at him. There was a bullet hole down through his collarbone. His face was gray with shock, but he had a very faint pulse. I yelled up the slope for someone to bring down my medical pouches. One of the riflemen did and helped me drag the boy down to where my eye patient lay. Aside from placing him in shock position, with his feet higher than his head, I didn't know what to do.

Shulman returned with litter bearers and our young aid station doctor. From what I witnessed, this doctor must have been rushed through medical school to supply the army. He was brave enough to come up to where the shooting was, but I don't think he knew much about doctoring. He hadn't brought the plasma I requested and didn't carry a physician's emergency medical pouch. He pronounced my frightened soldier dead. I told him the boy still had a pulse. He didn't check it; he told me I was feeling the pulse in my own fingertips. I was no doctor, but I knew a pulse when I felt one.

The doctor looked under the bandage of my eye patient, clucked his tongue, and had the litter bearers haul him away. I was mad as hell at that doctor. But my frightened boy was now the doctor's responsibility. A burst of machine gun fire told me the war was still on. I hated to leave that boy, but what could I do?

I cut across the mountain slope to find my CP. The fellows I had just taken care of didn't have a walkie-talkie with them, so they couldn't have been the ones who put in the call to Blackie. I had to find the right men. Now there were plenty of olive trees for cover. I hadn't gone far when a voice called, "Doc! Doc!"

I looked around but didn't see anyone. "Over here, Doc!" Five yards above me was a lieutenant huddled in a hollow tree trunk. His voice trembled. "Doc, some of my men are wounded up there!" He pointed straight up. I asked, "How many?" He was in tears. "Three. One is dead. A mortar got all of them. I was there . . ."

I went up to him and asked him to show me, but he was paralyzed with fear. He blurted, "I can't! They're straight up from here." He buried his face in his hands and sobbed. I never told anyone about this lieutenant—never mentioned it until now. I'm not a doctor, but I respected the confidentiality of every soldier I treated. At the end of the Sicily campaign I was informed that this lieutenant had asked to be relieved of duty and was transferred out of the company.

I scrambled straight up. These were probably the wounded I had first been called for. Now the mountain was terraced like big dirt steps—about ten- or fifteen-foot treads with five- or six-foot risers. A machine gun cut the air above me. Between bursts I scrambled over the step and across to the next riser. That German had me targeted, and dirt flecks from his bullets were coming closer. This guy did not show respect for my armband as the other German had done.

I'd gone about a hundred feet to a protected spot when two

litter bearers from my aid station came over a rise on my left. I called to them to follow me, and they came without hesitation. Now the machine gun that had gone silent came at us with a vengeance, kicking up dirt all around. The litter bearers were gone when I turned to look at them. Fearing they'd been hit, I yelled down, "Hey!"

One popped his head up from three terraces down and yelled, "We ain't comin' no more! They're shootin' at us!"

I blew my top. Exasperated, I yelled, "What the hell do you expect! Go on back and send me somebody who will come!"

To their credit, they hoisted their litter and came. The machine gun stopped firing, and we climbed for several minutes. The sun blazed, and my shirt was sticky with sweat. We finally came across two wounded men—Ewartz and Jones. They lay within arm's length of each other. A third boy, a little farther up, lay with his face turned into the dirt. He was dead.

The litter bearers found shelter while I worked on the wounded. One had a bullet low in his spine. After I patched him, he wanted to get up and walk. A litter bearer helped me get him erect, but he toppled over. He was not in pain—there's no pain with a severed spinal cord. The litter bearers took him down.

The second boy had a broken leg. Just as I finished rifle-splinting the leg and was wondering how I was going to get him down, Cowboy Wisecarver arrived with a rifleman and a litter bearer. The four of us took turns, two at a time, on the steep haul. I don't know why the German machine gun was suddenly silent.

The litter bearer began bitching. Cowboy shut him up with a menacing look and a few good words. A guy didn't mess around with Cowboy.

At the bottom of the mountain I hoped for a little rest. Voices from the road below came up to our company CP. Some officer said, "There are too goddamn many of 'em up there, Major. They're all over the ridge! How about air cover?" The answer was, "I tried, but they said the target is too small." The major continued, "I'm going to get the artillery to blast them!"

Blackie was on the road with his walkie-talkie. I heard him call up for all riflemen to come down. Apparently the message got through, because riflemen, silent and angry-looking, filtered down.

Before the barrage started, we were given a canteen of water and K rations. Cowboy Wisecarver came over to me and said, "There's a wounded man on the mountain over there." He pointed in the direction where I'd left the frightened soldier that our doctor had declared dead. When I questioned him, Cowboy said, "I saw him move." He guided me to the "wounded" boy. He was the same one, all right, but he was turned completely around from the shock position I'd left him in. Now he was dead.

Back in the CP a sergeant from the 2nd Platoon frantically appealed to our captain: "Damn it, sir! Sergeant Gregory is still up there with some of his men. They're pinned down by a machine gun, and he can't get out with his wounded. Our own barrage will hit them!" "The barrage has already been ordered," our captain said. "I can't stop it now. They'll have to take their chances."

The artillery barrage started low and rolled upward. My platoon, having been in reserve before, was first. We went up under the barrage. On my right a wiry, bowlegged private, Charles Kroetsching (soon after to become my best friend), eyed the top of the mountain and mumbled, "Count your men, you sons of bitches!"

We went up fast—too fast! Fragments from our own artillery hit some of our most forward men. As always, I was at the tail of my platoon. Sergeant Kennefac was on one side of me, and our captain was on the other. I stopped for two riflemen sitting on the ground. One had a pile of puke between his legs (he'd eaten all his rations before the attack). The second guy just sat there groaning and asked me if I had an aspirin. Fer cryin' out loud! In the middle of an attack? I didn't have an aspirin handy, but I gave him a bicarb pill. He didn't know the difference and went on his way. Two walking wounded came down to me as I started up. I patched them and sent them down. Kennefac had waited for me, and we went fast to catch the platoon.

I had to stop again when Private Shulman (who'd helped me with my eye patient earlier) scrambled down wincing with pain. His right hand had been shattered by a bullet. As I bandaged him, he said, "Sergeant Gregory is still up there with some fellows and two wounded. Bastards broke my rifle. Going to get another one and be right back . . ." Shulman stumbled on down past me. I never saw him again.

Kennefac was still with me, but our captain had disappeared. The barrage was deafening. We climbed fast until we saw the tail end of our platoon as it vanished over a terrace. Then the barrage came to a sudden halt.

Second Platoon Technical Sergeant Gregory came sliding down to me. "Got a wounded man up here, Doc. Can you take a look at him?" It wasn't a question. Gregory was away before I could open my mouth. Kennefac went on ahead. I followed and caught Gregory a few steps from his men, who were huddled against a terrace step. A German machine gun opened up on us—the first return fire since the barrage ended. Gregory and I took a flying dive and banged against the terrace riser.

The machine gun traversed the edge of the step and showered dirt on us. Then their mortars screamed down—four in rapid succession that exploded with brain-pounding concussion just above our heads. A couple more feet and we'd have all been dead. We all froze in complete silence. Maybe the Germans thought they'd killed us, because they threw no more mortars.

When the dust cleared, I saw there were six of us, including Gregory's wounded man. No one moved or spoke for fear of bringing down more shells. I crawled to the wounded man, who lay on his stomach. He had four bullet holes within inches in his lower back. Intestine or fatty tissue seeped out when I cut away his shirt. I sprinkled sulfa powder and tied a large Carlisle bandage tight to keep in whatever was coming out. When the man winced with pain, I gave him a whole morphine syrette.

Strangely, there was a blanket handy. Someone said Shulman had left it. Few of us carried blankets in the hot Sicilian summer. I covered my patient to help prevent shock, then lay as still as he did.

Our barrage hadn't pulverized the Germans. Rifle and machine gun fire banged away all over the mountain above. It wasn't long before night settled in, and Gregory went scouting below to assess our situation. Isolated, we didn't know who had the mountain or if we'd be caught in a counterattack.

Gregory returned; the mountain below us was clear. He wanted to fix a makeshift litter to take the wounded man down. I didn't like the idea of a rough litter haul, since I didn't know what kind of internal damage might cause hemorrhage. I just felt it would be better if a regular litter team with a good litter took the boy down.

Gregory didn't want to leave his man, but I finally persuaded him to go. I'd stay with him and wait for morning evacuation. It later turned out that my instincts were right. As the war progressed, doctors agreed that moving a wounded man too fast could lead to shock. As long as he was in a safe place, it was best for him to stay where he was and rest.

Gregory waited a bit longer for the night to get blacker. He gave me an abandoned rifle with two clips of ammo. "This is all I can spare," he whispered. "I've used up most of my ammo." The rifle he gave me had a bayonet stuck on it, and I do mean "stuck." I couldn't get it off. Gregory and his men faded into the night below.

I sat next to my patient with my back against the terrace. A German machine gun above me shattered the quiet with harassing fire. After every short burst, the character on the machine gun laughed like a maniac. He might have been high on something. Where I was, I felt safe enough from the machine gun—it was the crazy laughing that got on my nerves. I'm no tough guy, but the longer that bastard laughed, the madder I got. I decided to go after the son of a bitch. I snapped one of my eight-shot clips into the M1, tried again to take off the bayonet—no luck—and started up over the riser, only to get blown down by the first explosion from a night artillery barrage—ours. Wow! That took all the fight out of me.

Along with the 105-mm and 155-mm artillery shells, we were throwing 4.2-inch chemical mortars. Their phosphorus set fire to brush all around me. I was above the tree line, however, and there was no real fire danger, since the scraggly brush was thin and spread out.

The shells continued to scream in and explode deafeningly. I had the confidence born of ignorance that our own artillery couldn't possibly hit me, but I did hope it would take out that German machine gun above me. It didn't. As soon as the barrage stopped, the machine gun and the crazy laughter continued.

I didn't know what time it was when the mountain finally quieted down and the phosphorus fires burned out. A thick black silence settled in. Even the German was quiet. My patient had slept through the barrages thanks, probably, to the morphine I had given him. Now he stirred under the blanket and murmured, "Gregory?" I patted him lightly on the shoulder but didn't speak for fear he wouldn't recognize my voice. He fell back into a deep sleep.

I tried to stay awake but fell asleep sitting up. I woke when I fell over. The mountain was deathly still. Clouds that had obscured the stars had vanished, and they seemed close enough to touch. I shivered in the cold mountain air and eyed the blanket over my motionless patient. I thought he was probably dead, so I pulled the blanket off him and covered myself. Then I had a guilty conscience. Maybe he wasn't dead. I lay alongside him and pulled half the blanket over him.

I lay with the rifle at my side and pillowed my head in my arms. My sleeves stank from dried blood. I'd been running up and down that damn mountain all day, and I was exhausted. I fell asleep again.

Some strange warning in my subconscious roused me to full wakefulness. Dawn was starting to trickle down the mountain. Every instinct said danger! From below came the sound of someone climbing. I grabbed my rifle, flipped off the safety, and aimed at the noise. As my finger tensed on the trigger, a GI helmet appeared. When the fellow came into full view, I yelled, "Get down!" He dropped, then got up and looked at me queerly. I waved him back to the ground and yelled, "There's a machine gun up there!"

He came to me saying, "What the hell's the matter with you? We took this mountain a couple of hours ago! I'm looking for the mortar OP (observation post). Seen it?"

I shook my head, dumbfounded, and he went up. The "corpse" at my side rose on one elbow and said, "You know, . . . I feel pretty good."

I checked his bandages, and for the first time since attacking the mountain, I reviewed what had happened. When I bandaged Shulman, he'd said there were *two* wounded men with Gregory. Gregory hadn't said anything about another one—probably too much on his mind. When I asked my patient, he said, "Someone was hit down there." He pointed down the mountain to the left.

I scrambled down to look and found the wounded boy within a hundred feet. Aid station Corporal Frank Riccata was there ahead of me, splinting two legs broken below the knees—machine gun slugs. I helped Frank.

The wounded boy was angry with me. "Where were you? I called all night!" I felt terrible. I hadn't heard him or I would have taken care of him. With the machine gun above me and the artillery barrage, I just didn't know he was there.

I liked Frank Riccata. Aside from First Sergeant Leon Shapley and him, I didn't know much about the aid station men. I only went there to replenish my supplies. When Riccata and I finished splinting the boy, I took him up to see my gut-shot patient. Frank told me he'd see to the evacuation and gave me his full canteen of water for my empty one.

I staggered up the mountain to look for my company. A signalman, running a wire downhill, told me that I Company was near the top. I sighed with relief, slumped at the base of a shattered, solitary tree, and fell asleep. But I didn't get much rest. Every few minutes a passing rifleman shook me to find out if I was dead.

When I finally got to I Company, it was resting at the crest of the mountain. I plopped down by one of the company medics, Dorsey Tash, and was so exhausted I could hardly breathe. With a gasp, I asked Tash for a Benzedrine pill. (Mine had vanished from my pouches, either lost or stolen.) That little pill so stimulated me that when, within the hour, we got a call to "saddle up!" I half carried a rifleman and his pack up to a town at the top of the mountain and through it to a meadow on the far side. We were told we could rest for a couple of hours, but I couldn't sleep, though I was dying to. I never again took Benzedrine.

Earlier on the slope, Lieutenant Barker had asked me to look at his foot. My god! He had blisters that had broken on new blisters, so that the ball of his foot was raw flesh the size of a silver dollar. I applied my famous blister bandage—sulfa powder, cotton wrapped in a three-inch bandage, and the whole thing taped down with wide adhesive tape.

When I asked Barker how his water supply was, he thought I was asking for some, and he apologized. When we got rations before attacking the mountain, he'd passed out all the water to the men and had none for himself. He'd been without water for almost two days. I told him I had a full canteen from the aid station, and he took a good swig. "Doc" he said, "that was worth a hundred dollars!" (In Depression money, that was a lot!)

When we went through the mountaintop city, natives told us that every German who passed through in retreat was carrying a wounded man or helping to carry one. Our night barrage had caught them as they were retreating, and they were too far from their holes to get back. Tech Sergeant Martinez told me he'd been on top, where our barrage caught the retreating Germans: "They lay dead in groups of twos and threes all over the place." I didn't see it myself.

The next morning we started down the mountain to the Mediterranean coast. Ten men from a company ahead of us had been killed. A friendly Sicilian had warned them that a small bridge was mined, but the lead officer scoffed and led his men across. It was mined.

We were warned away from ditches and shady spots where we'd be inclined to rest. Orders were passed, "Stay on the road! Watch for booby traps! Don't pick anything up!"

We got down to the coastal road with no more casualties. That evening the 3rd Infantry Division passed through us. We sat along the cliff side of the Mediterranean road as they passed. They hadn't been in action and strode with fresh, springy steps, bodies erect. They made me realize just how low our asses were dragging, but they were a careless lot. They smoked glowing cigarettes, and their trucks moved bumper to bumper with blackout lights show-ing. Sergeant Matthews called, "Put out your light! The Germans are just down the road a little piece!" An insolent voice called back, "Hell, man, we're the famous 3rd Division! Haven't you heard of us?"

We heard about them the next morning after they'd had the hell strafed out of them by German planes.

Lieutenant Evans informed us we were going back for a rest near Palermo. We believed it when we boarded trucks that took us all the way back along the Mediterranean coast. It was late when we pulled into an olive grove on a cliff overlooking the Mediterranean. We got to sleep late and were aroused by the call, "Come and get it!"

Our company kitchen truck had set up within fifty yards of where I slept, and we were about to get our first hot meal since the landing. We had been on the go for twenty-one continuous days without rest.

We ate by platoons. As always, I was bringing up the rear of mine when the call "Medic!" came from the kitchen truck area. I raced forward, thinking someone was injured. When I got the head of the food line, Sergeant Kennefac was laughing and said, "Doc, you eat first!"

It took a while for it to sink in that I was being honored for my work at Castel de Tusa and "Bloody Ridge." I didn't know our own aid station men, but one came over to my slit trench and gave me a haircut. Another took my hunting knife and put a razor edge on it. A correspondent from *Stars and Stripes* came to interview me, but I didn't want to talk about myself. Our company runner Henry Fisk asked if there was anything he could do for me: "Dig your slit trench?"

A new platoon lieutenant, Jake Blumberg, came to tell me that the officers had had a meeting and I'd been given complete author-ity in any medical matters. That was my status with I Company throughout my year of combat with it.

A few days later, Lieutenant Blumberg asked if I'd go on a mis-sion. The regiment was going to make an end run around the

Germans a few miles before Messina. Blumberg was going to take an advance squad of twelve men to be first ashore to cut wire on the beach. I volunteered.

On August 18, 1943, we made the landing, but it turned out the Germans had already gone past the point of our landing, with the 3rd Division in hot pursuit. However, the Germans crossed over the Strait of Messina to the toe of Italy. Our 1st Battalion got into Messina before the 3rd Division. If Patton, or somebody, had had one destroyer in the Strait, we might have wiped out what we had to fight all over again in Italy.

We rested until the end of August.

Just before we invaded Italy, we were back at Palermo. Lieutenant General George S. Patton Jr. came into our area and addressed the division's officers and noncoms. The gist of his talk was, "Throw away your shovels, men! We're just going in there and chase them!" We looked at each other as if he were nuts. We weren't riding big steel tanks. We needed our shovels. Where we went was to the invasion of Italy—Salerno! (More exactly— Paestum!)

3

The Invasion of Italy

SEPTEMBER 1943

The Battle of Salerno (about twenty-five miles south of Naples) was not fought at Salerno. It was fought in the fields of Paestum, about fifteen to twenty miles south of Salerno.

On the morning of September 9, 1943, three German bombers droned high over our massed invasion fleet. They were so high they looked like specks in the sky, and they seemed harmless until the sea erupted in a tremendous geyser about fifty yards from the LCI (landing craft infantry) that I Company was aboard.

The long and narrow LCI had a ladder on each side of the bow for disembarking men when the ship plowed onto the beach. It had a housing amidships, with a 20-mm gun on top. The whole crew was British, and the sailor manning the gun sported a beautiful red beard.

While Red Beard leaned against his gun and gazed skyward, a new lieutenant we'd taken on after the Sicily campaign jumped up and down as a second bomb whipped up the sea. He shouted, "Goddamnit! Don't you see him? Shoot! Shoot!"

Red Beard stroked his beautiful beaver, glanced down at the lieutenant, up at the German plane, then down at the lieutenant again. "Lieutenant," he calmly said, "'e's too bloody 'igh!"

News of Italy's surrender was announced while we were on the sea en route. We assumed there'd be no fighting, that it would indeed be just a "chase 'em," as we'd done in Sicily. We couldn't have been more wrong. We didn't know that the Germans had taken complete military control of all Italy.[1]

There was no advance artillery or air bombardment when, on the morning of September 9, the 36th Division led the first waves of troops onto the beach. We later heard that the Germans had just finished "repelling invasion maneuvers" on the beaches where the 36th landed. Parts of the 36th Division were blown out of the water. Troops that made it ashore were surrounded and captured or annihilated.

We didn't know how serious the situation was. The invasion of Italy might have been a major disaster if it hadn't been for our two regiments of the 45th Division, the 157th and the 179th. (Our third regiment, the 180th, was still in Sicily for lack of transport. The 2nd Battalion of the 157th was left in Sicily in reserve.) The British had landed on the toe and heel of Italy and wouldn't arrive at Paestum for a week.

We went in on the second morning and again had the good fortune to land on an undefended beach. The sea was calm, but tragedy struck when some of the LCIs around us prematurely dropped their bow ladders and off-loaded the troops when they hit underwater sandbars. Our skipper saw the problem and rammed through the sandbars. As we went past, I could see dozens of rifles held out of the water, while the men holding them were completely submerged. Many must have drowned.

Moments before our LCI hit the beach, it dropped its anchor. The ladders went down, and we went ashore high and dry. The LCI hauled in its anchor and pulled itself off the beach.

I had a fever that morning. Another boy also had a fever, much worse than mine. I told him to stay in his bunk and go back with

1. After the Allied victory in Sicily, King Victor Emmanuel III engaged in secret negotiations with the Allies and arranged for Italy to drop out of the Axis, request an armistice, and bring his country over to the American and British side. Italian dictator Benito Mussolini was removed from power on July 24, 1943, and Marshal Pietro Badoglio was appointed to form a new government. On September 8, 1943, as the invasion force was steaming toward Salerno, Italy's surrender was officially announced. The Allies hoped that news of the capitulation would cause Hitler to withdraw his forces and abandon Italy, but the opposite occurred: the Germans decided to stay and fight. Some Italian military units chose to serve under Allied command, and others cast their lot with the Germans. Martin Blumenson, *United States Army in World War II: The Mediterranean Theater of Operations—Salerno to Cassino* (Washington DC: Office of the Chief of Military History, 1967), 16–26, 41, 43.

the ship. I never carried a thermometer. I would judge a fever by checking a man's pulse against my own. If I was sick and the man's pulse was even faster than mine, I knew he was sicker than I was. If his pulse was faster than mine when I was normal, then he had a fever. Simple.

Within minutes of our landing, German shells began exploding on the beach. With the first explosion, my fever vanished. As we raced off the beach, I stopped to help a machine gunner whose heavy ammo cart was sunk to its hubs in the sand. Together we dragged it to firm ground. That cart should have had runners like skis to slide across the sand.

My platoon was sprawled among scrawny bushes and trees. Our Spitfires and P-38s screamed over the treetops, heading out to sea. Their markings were clear—and what idiot could mistake a P-38 for an Me-109? Ships at sea began firing at our planes as succeeding waves of them roared overhead. Trigger-happy riflemen got the shooting fever from the ships. Sergeant Matthews and I ran from hole to hole yelling, "Hold your fire! They're *our* planes!"

Not more than three hours passed, and while we were marching up a tree-lined road, we were read a memo from the air corps: "This morning, ground troops and ships at sea destroyed ten of our aircraft. The air corps will stop supporting the ground forces until the ground forces stop shooting down our planes!"

Green pastures rolled away from each side of the road. In one field several beautiful horses frolicked, their manes and tails flying.

High in the clear sky, a P-51 and a German plane were tangled in a dogfight. The air was filled with the whine of their dives and the pullout roar of their motors. Wings flashed fire and, unexpectedly late, the rat-a-tat-tat of their guns floated down to us while the planes were going in opposite directions. The German peeled off on one wing and spiraled down, followed by a trickle of smoke. Soon the trickle became a heavy black trail that streaked the sky long after the German plane disappeared.

It was late afternoon when the company halted. I don't know where we were. We had passed the excavated ruins of an ancient

Roman city—Paestum—very much like the ruins I later saw at Pompeii. Lieutenant Blumberg volunteered the platoon to knock out a German roadblock "up ahead a piece."

Soon after dark, my platoon gathered on the road. There was a popping noise and some sparks, and someone yelled, "Grenade!" Clarence Jones had accidentally pulled the pin of a grenade hanging from his pack strap. He barely got it away from himself, and it exploded where he threw it in a roadside ditch. Two men were slightly wounded—a calf wound and an arm wound.

Sergeant Matthews checked the men. Everyone answered except Private Bove, who suddenly appeared from the water-filled ditch. He gasped, "Ma-an, wha-at h-happened?" He wasn't wounded, but he was soaked to the skin.

Instead of forty, we were now thirty-eight men . . . nineteen striding up each side of the road. Sergeant Kennefac brought up the end of one column, and I brought up the end of the other . . . three BARs, three grenade-launching '03s, a tommy gun, a bazooka, and the rest MIs. It grew so dark I couldn't see where we were going, but in front of me was Private Bombard with his bazooka. It made a clanking noise, and that's what I followed. A solitary German machine gun chattered from far up the road—harassing fire.

It seemed as if we'd gone a quarter mile from our starting point, and we hadn't run into a roadblock. A long stretch of elevated road passed over a meadow, with a three-foot concrete rail bordering each side. The machine gun cut loose again—closer. I instinctively folded into the ground. Silence. At the center of the elevated road, men slipped over the rail, about a six-foot drop. Our two columns had now become one. I had no sooner hit the ground than I heard a sharp pop overhead. Kennefac called "Freeze!" The pop was a flare that turned the night to day. I was halfway to the ground and froze in a crouch. I guess we looked like clumps of brush; the machine gun didn't cut us down.

As soon as the flare went out, we ran back and spread out in a bush-covered dry ravine we had just crossed. Our rifles were at the ready, but nothing happened. Corporal Moreno lay on one side of me and Ted Slifer on the other. Near Moreno was a scared rifleman who whimpered, "Let's get out of here." Moreno warned him twice to shut up, then shut him up with a hard kick to his ass.

Lieutenant Blumberg, with Sergeant Matthews and Sergeant Kennefac, disappeared across the meadow to scout our situation. I was forever puzzled about how they could see where they were going in the dark. They were back within a half hour. "No roadblock—only found a couple of German graves."

Private Henry Fisk was sent back to find out what the regiment wanted us to do. It was almost an hour before he got back, so I slept while he was gone. Fisk returned with orders to reconnoiter a secondary road that swung left off the road we'd been on. The night grew blacker than ever. I just followed Bombard's bazooka.[2] My eyes finally became accustomed to the dark, and I could make out a line of men ahead of me. We slipped past a large farmhouse and barn, cut across a barbed-wire-enclosed pasture, followed a bush-lined creek, and crossed the creek on a fallen tree. The field broadened, free of trees and brush, but soggy.

Now our thirty-eight men formed a long line of skirmishers. I followed at the center to watch for stragglers. The broad field ended in a row of tall trees. Now, single file, we filtered through a short stretch of cow path and were again in a soggy field. Our shoes made sucking noises in the muck.

"Halt!" came a guttural voice ahead.

The line of men flopped into the mud—all except me and Clarence Jones. I didn't feel like getting muddy. Clarence Jones, alongside me, reared back with his grenade launcher—prepared to fire.

"Pass one!" the guttural voice commanded.

Sergeant Kennefac recovered even before Lieutenant Blumberg. "Baca," he ordered. "You're first scout! Go!"

2. The bazooka, an antitank shoulder weapon, fired a high-explosive rocket that damaged a German tank only if it hit the treads. I've seen it bounce off tank turrets with no obvious damage. It took its name from a "musical instrument" used by radio and movie comedian Bob Burns in the 1930s. Burns made it from a pipe and a funnel and played it somewhat like a trombone. He called the instrument "my bazooka," and the name stuck for the tinny device that became our rifleman-carried rocket weapon.

Mike Baca rose from the mud and disappeared in the dark. Crouching low, I moved over to a dry dirt path on my right. I erroneously thought that if I couldn't see the "German," he couldn't see me. Lieutenant Blumberg was only a few feet from me on the path. I found that out when Mike Baca called, "Lieutenant Blumberg, forward!"

It was so dark I didn't know Blumberg was only a few feet from my side until he rose and went forward. Within a few minutes all the men got up and went forward. I hadn't heard any orders to move, but I didn't want to get left behind, so I went forward too.

A scant few yards ahead, a small group of GIs was clustered around a British Bren gunner[3] in a standing foxhole. Only his head was above ground. What I had thought was a German accent was a British accent with a heavy cold behind it. I gave the guy a couple of aspirins.

This was the first we knew that some British were at Paestum ahead of us. "Been 'ere two days," the Britisher said. "'ave some Bren guns set up across the field back there and got orders to 'old this line." It was only a small unit of British.

Lieutenant Blumberg came back after consulting with British officers. A German machine gun erupted suddenly. I hit the ground.

The British soldier with the cold calmly said, "No need worrying about 'im, 'e's on an 'ill up there. Only 'arassing." Blumberg turned to Kennefac. "Maybe we ought to go after him." "You can do it easy," the Britisher prompted. "We been a bit short 'anded, but you got more than enough men." Blumberg consulted further with Kennefac and Matthews. They decided that since it was near dawn, we'd better get back to the battalion.

We retraced our steps through the night. Dawn was breaking when we reached the place on the main road where we had left the battalion. It wasn't there! It had pulled back without sending us word, and we were angry until we found out later that a whole

3. The British Bren gun was the equivalent of our light .30-caliber machine gun. There always seemed to be two or three British soldiers with each Bren gun. Cowboy Wisecarver of I Company handled his .30-caliber machine gun alone—and he was deadly with it.

German panzer division had pulled into the field opposite. We'd gone right through them during the night without knowing it.

When we finally caught up with battalion, Blumberg and Kennefac went to find the command post. Matthews led us into a field that had three shade trees. I plopped down under one and fell asleep.

German shells exploding at the far end of our field awakened me, and I started digging a slit trench. A terrified medic from our nearby aid station came running toward me. He was really wild— just running crazy out of his mind. I remembered this guy's telling me how he had screwed an innocent young girl in a lumberyard near his home. I disliked men who boasted about their sexual conquests, and now this guy really showed his true colors. He went past me and disappeared in a clump of trees.

Explosions came closer. Kennefac came back with bad news. Our 1st Battalion was in serious trouble. I still hadn't seen a German soldier. Within a half hour we were hustled to a hidden motor pool, loaded up on about ten trucks, and taken on a wild five-minute ride. We off-loaded behind a row of trees not far from the beach, then we hiked into an open field and spread out near a deserted farmhouse. Nearby, a battery of 4.2 mortars fired a barrage of shells. I asked one of the crew what they were firing at. His one-word response: "Tanks!"

Having been in such a hurry, we sat around for an hour. Nothing happened. Our kitchen truck sent up jelly sandwiches, and I fought yellow jackets that swarmed to the jelly. I just brushed them off without getting stung.

Finally the company formed and marched off on a diagonal across the field in front of the farmhouse. The field ended at the edge of a twenty-foot cliff, and the trail leading down brought us into a beautiful grassy meadow. Across the meadow a stream bordered a forest. Our cliff wall was covered with a dense growth of leafy bushes, and we dug in under them. The north end of the meadow, toward the Germans, was spanned by what seemed to be an ancient Roman aqueduct that had once connected two thirty-foot cliffs. The center of the aqueduct had been blown away, and water tumbled down into the stream opposite.

Next to a slit trench I dug was a very dejected mortar man. He told me he was part of three mortar crews that had set up in the meadow and were firing in support of troops in a cornfield beyond the aqueduct. Only a short time before we arrived, a German patrol had sneaked around through the opposite woods, set up a machine gun, and killed all the mortar men except him. "Some of our fellows from the cornfield doubled back and killed the Germans. Their bodies are still there by the trees." He couldn't understand how he was still alive while all his buddies were dead.

My good pal Charles Kroetsching slid down from the cliff. In each hand, and filling his combat jacket, were round green objects about the size of small cantaloupes. He laughed and sliced one open with his bayonet—they were ripe watermelons. I climbed up the cliff with Charles and, sure enough, little watermelons were growing all over the field. We brought down as many as we could carry and passed them out to the platoon.

There was no tent, so the 1st Battalion aid station was set up under a towering oak tree by the left side of the aqueduct. Wounded men were coming in from the cornfield—some by themselves, some aided by buddies, some on litters. After treatment, they were housed in a large cave in the cliff's base. A wounded sergeant came toward me half carrying a wounded buddy. He didn't look too good himself, and when I asked him if he was okay, he said, "Yeah . . . take care of my buddy." I took the wounded man to the doctor. When I went back to the sergeant, he lay on the ground—dead.

Our lieutenant called for grenade launchers and bazookas. I went up the cliff above the aid station where a squad, under Sergeant Hogate, was spread out in a natural defilade. Blumberg took only two men with him to scout the Germans, leaving the rest with Hogate.

Ahead and to our right below was the cornfield where the 1st Battalion was taking a beating. Ahead of us was an open field about a hundred yards across, where German shells began exploding. German tanks emerged from a line of trees several hundred yards to our left front. Exploding shells were coming closer.

We all lay prone except for Hogate. He stood erect and called fire orders to an artillery observer who remained below by the aid station because he was afraid to come up to us. The observer relayed the fire orders to our artillery. As our shells began exploding near the tanks, they withdrew to the shelter of their trees. The call "Medic!" came from about twenty yards to my left. In a deep erosion ditch were five men from an engineer party. One had an arm wound. After dressing it, I sent him down to the aid station.

No sooner was I back at Hogate's position than, seemingly from out of nowhere, three mud-covered riflemen, eyes wild with fright, raced through our defilade and down to the aid station below. They were hardly gone when a second lieutenant ran to us with the same frightened look. He shouted, "Get the hell out of here! They're coming!" and he was gone.

The same man Moreno had kicked in the ass the night before started up after the lieutenant. Hogate stopped him in his tracks. The scared boy cried, "Didn't you hear that lieutenant? He said to get out of here!"

Hogate pointed his rifle and clicked off the safety. "That guy ain't running this squad!" The scared boy went back to his position. The frightened GIs and the scared lieutenant panicked the aid station. The doctor and all the medics left their patients and scrambled up the cliff to where we were, saw they were headed in the wrong direction, and ran back down to the meadow.

Hogate squirted tobacco juice, shook his head in disgust, and muttered, "Can't see nothing to get excited about." There were no Germans coming at us.

Lieutenant Blumberg and his men withdrew from the field, where the tanks had come fairly close before our artillery caused them to retreat.

We returned to the meadow, now filled with the entire 3rd Battalion. Had the German artillery zeroed in on us, we'd have been slaughtered. Fortunately they didn't.

Orders came to pull back to our earlier position near the farmhouse. I Company stayed behind to cover the withdrawal. Artillery began exploding in the field above the meadow—seemingly our own or from the 36th Division, with whom we had no communication. The battalion got back with no casualties that I knew of. When my platoon, which was covering I Company's retreat, started back, we had to run back to the edge of the meadow cliff because shells were again exploding in the field. When the shelling stopped, we were prepared for a German advance through the meadow, but all that came were a few mud-covered riflemen from 1st Battalion. One plopped down near me to get his breath. "It's murder!" he gasped. "Murder! . . . They trapped us in a corn-field. Everybody's dead! Crawled through a muddy ditch and got away . . ." He staggered across the field after the others.

Everybody wasn't dead. One by one, survivors came up from the meadow and disappeared across the field. When dusk fell, we pulled back to I Company and dug in along a stretch of tall bushes. Word spread to us: "Colonel Ankcorn says this is as far back as we go. We're going to hold here!"

That night I went along with a twelve-man squad that Lieu-tenant Blumberg took on a reconnaissance. Supposedly a German scout car was running up and down the road between our com-panies. No one was challenging it.

Sure enough, the German scout car came from their lines as if it were joy-riding. Blumberg said we'd take it on its way back. Bombard was supposed to knock it out with his bazooka, but the damn thing wouldn't fire. The car would have gotten away except for Clarence Jones. He blew off a front wheel with his grenade launcher.[4] We captured three dazed Germans. Blumberg told Moreno to take the Germans to the rear, but Moreno wanted to kill them. "What if they don't get back?" he said angrily.

Blumberg said quietly, "See that they do," and Moreno took off with them. Sometimes he acted tougher than he really was. He had told me that on Bloody Ridge in Sicily he came upon a German communications wire and cut it. Then he lay prone on the German end and sighted along his rifle. Pretty soon there was a tugging as a German came checking for the break. But when the man came into full view, Moreno didn't have the heart to kill

---

4. The muzzle of the '03 Springfield rifle was fitted with an attachment to secure a concussion grenade that was launched with a blank cartridge. The grenade exploded on contact.

him in cold blood. The German saw Moreno, jumped away, and was gone.

On September 14, 1943, the Germans began their major offensive to wipe us out. The morning broke clear and sunny. A barrage of German shells exploded in the field ahead of us. There were a lot of duds among the screaming incoming shells, maybe because they were armor-piercing and soft dirt didn't set them off. Maybe they were sabotaged in slave labor factories in Germany. Who knows?

Enough did go off to cause damage. Mendoza, one of our scouts from another platoon, got out of his slit trench for some unknown reason, and an exploding shell killed him. On Bloody Ridge in Sicily, Mendoza had come across a mortally wounded German and put him out of his misery.

A cow munching in the field looked fine one minute, and the next it was on its back without a head. I could look through the severed neck into the cow's body cavity. The carcass bloated rapidly in the sun.

One man from my platoon dived alongside my slit trench. He said, "Damn new lieutenant kept diving into my slit trench every time a shell came in. I told him to dig his own hole. A minute ago a shell hit the edge of my hole but didn't go off! We were nose to nose! I got the hell out of there! The lieutenant can have the hole!"

Lieutenant Blumberg's slit trench was near mine, but he sat outside it and doodled in the dirt. Each time a shell exploded, he asked me where it had landed. When they got too close, he said, "Well, better get in my hole." It was the first time I realized Blumberg couldn't see farther than a few hundred feet. I never told anyone.

Blumberg explained Colonel Ankcorn's defensive setup. Our companies were entrenched under tall windbreak trees along three fields. We were in the shape of a large U, with companies along the legs of the U. I Company extended along the base of the U and beyond the legs to form a trap. No matter which way the Germans came at us, they came under fire from two or three directions. In front of us was a huge gully that was a natural tank barrier. To protect our left and right flanks, we had our own tanks and field artillery. I do believe that during the next few days of fighting, the Germans never could figure out where we were.

On our second night Blumberg took a patrol to check out a berserk lieutenant. When we got to him, he seemed completely out of his head. He had positioned his decimated platoon and gone scouting. The platoon moved from its position, and when the lieutenant got back he couldn't find anyone. He was out of his mind worrying about them. Blumberg finally got him to go back to headquarters by telling him the colonel wanted a personal report.

On my platoon's left flank was part of I Company and our 179th Regiment, which was in a seesaw battle over a tobacco factory. The position was vital to our flank protection. Each time we took the factory, the Germans counterattacked and took it back. Eventually, George Hogate told me, he was sent out there with a large backpack radio. He watched several German command cars pull in around the building, and when he thought there were enough of them inside, he called in an artillery barrage that blew the place apart.

On the third day the Germans came at us with massed infantry. The GIs along the tree lines cut them down, with no casualties to us that I knew of. I heard no calls of "Medic!" When the Germans attacked our right they ran into fire from the "wedge." When they tried to outflank the wedge, they attacked into the "box" and were cut down from three sides.

Johnny Matthews and Kennefac had been sent on a mission by regimental headquarters to scout out opposition across the field and down to the meadow and beyond. They carried backpack radios and were supposed to call back information from over two miles into German territory. These were men I admired, and I worried about them. They had been gone two days. I was lying in Matthews's slit trench, concealed under thick bushes, because for some reason it gave me comfort to be there. Matthews had left a Charlie Chan pocket book. I was flat on my back reading it when the Germans attacked into the box. The volume of small-arms fire was unbelievable. Rifle and machine gun bullets cut through the bushes above my head and sheared off a blanket of leaves that fell on me. I felt secure in Matthews's foot-deep slit trench, and I tried to see the bullets as they cut the leaves. Nope. Just falling leaves.

Before this attack, while I was still in my own hole, which was getting a little deeper and bigger each day, two riflemen from the 36th Division found their way into my platoon CP. They were bewildered and hadn't the faintest notion of where their outfit was. One said, "We dug slit trenches in a field and settled down for the night. Pretty soon everybody is shooting the shit out of us. Tanks and panzer troops were on top of us, but it was so dark we couldn't see what to shoot at, and nobody was giving us orders about what to do! We came across a staff sergeant who had just shot a lieutenant . . . said the guy was talking German into a walkie-talkie. We sneaked off into the woods and finally worked our way over here." The two joined my platoon and dug slit trenches.

The fourth morning, I slung my gear and told Lieutenant Blumberg I was going out to the meadow to look for Matthews and Kennefac. While I was talking to Blumberg, Matthews walked into the CP! He and Kennefac had returned the night before and spent it at regimental headquarters. I was so relieved that I kissed Matthews on both cheeks like a Frenchman, which made him blush. That night Kennefac was sent out into the battlefield of the box to get information from dead Germans. When he got back he told me he hated touching the dead, but he did bring back information about who we were fighting—the Hermann Göring Division that we had been chasing in Sicily.

Thereafter, each night Mike Baca, Baide Black, Ted Slifer, and Sergeant Kennefac took turns sneaking out into "no-man's-land." They dug standing foxholes, and with telephones in hand, waited tensely to send word of a night attack. But it seemed that the Germans preferred to sleep at night. In addition, they had suffered such serious casualties during their daytime attacks that they seemed to have had their fill of us. Things were quiet after the fourth and fifth days.

I went on a final patrol with Blumberg. A GI on our left flank was loudly challenging something in the field ahead of him. When we got near, he was shouting, "Stop or I'll shoot!" At the sound of us, he whirled and fired. Fortunately he didn't hit anyone. What he was challenging was *a cow munching in the field!*

Strange things happened at Paestum. A German fighter plane was shot down near us. The plane made a successful emergency landing—and the pilot was a woman.[5] She surprised everyone when she took off her headgear and shook out her hair.

Another strange event: Our "division bomber" (a Piper Cub) regularly flew overhead as observer for the artillery. One of our shells hit the plane in midair. The pilot disappeared in the explosion.

The most tragic event occurred when we were warned to be on the lookout for German paratroopers. Sure enough, that afternoon the sky was filled with paratroopers. The infantry shot them all down . . . only they were Americans. I met one of the survivors when I was in an African hospital, a medic who made that jump. He told me he had several bullet wounds when he landed, but all the men who landed around him were dead.

One event was like a Mac Sennett movie comedy. An antiaircraft gun had been moved into the bushes near my slit trench. Three men were supposed to operate it: one cranked it left and one cranked it right while the third man was supposed to fire it. When a German fighter plane screamed in low overhead, the three characters were so excited they didn't man the gun—they didn't know how. They argued about who was supposed to do what. No way in the world were they going to hit an Me-109 going past at 350 miles an hour. They were gone the morning after they arrived.

I was called to our left flank, where one of our men lay unconscious on open ground. He trembled from head to foot, and saliva dribbled from his mouth. "He's been pretty scared," one of the platoon members said.

5. This woman was probably one of those who transported planes to various destinations, just as American woman pilots did. According to Reina Pennington's book *Amazon to Fighter Pilots,* the Germans had only two women who flew fighters as test pilots: Hanna Reitsch and Melitta Stuffenberg.

I gave the boy a whiff of spirits of ammonia. His eyes fluttered open, and he moaned, "Don't let them get me! Don't let them get me!" When one of our own shells screamed overhead, he passed out again. Spirits of ammonia again, and the same terror, until the next passing shell made him unconscious again. I flagged down a passing jeep and sent the boy to the rear.

One morning while bullets were flying and shells were exploding, Sterling Johnson, our company clerk, risked his life to bring us—of all things—mail!

I had a letter from an old school friend who was in Australia. He wrote, "You're lucky to be where the action is. I have an office full of girl typists, and they want to stop for tea three times a day. I can't get the work done!"

On a more peaceful day, I wrote back, "I'll be glad to trade places with you, and I'll serve the girls tea every hour on the hour and serve it personally." (He wound up marrying a very lovely Australian girl.)

When he got mail, Lieutenant Blumberg was so elated he was about to burst. Since I was the medic, he confided in me. "Look," he said, waving his letter. "My girlfriend says she still loves me!" Blumberg and his girl had had a spat before he left the States, and she'd called off their engagement. No wonder he was volunteering for everything and sitting outside his hole during barrages. I guess he was trying to commit suicide. Now he couldn't contain his joy and showed me his girl's picture. Wow! Angel cake! After that Blumberg couldn't wait to win the war, and he continued to volunteer for everything. Trouble was, he also volunteered the platoon.

The last furious German infantry assault on the fifth day ended their effort to drive us into the sea. We didn't know it at the time, but the British coming up from the toe of Italy were about to flank them. We didn't know until the next morning that the Germans had pulled out in the night.

That morning the 3rd Division came ashore. One platoon straggled into our concealed position, drank from our precious water cans, took off their olive drab shirts to expose white undershirts, and generally acted like a training film on how to do everything wrong! I exploded and told them to get the hell out of our command post—that there were Germans across the field! A cocky private boasted, "Shit! Ain't you heard of us? We're the famous 3rd Division!" The smartass started to argue with me when I told him again to get the hell out of our CP. A 3rd Division sergeant who was looking us over told the private, "Shut your big mouth, and get the hell out of here like you're told!" then he turned to me, "Been pretty rough?" he asked. I told him.

Blumberg, Kennefac, and Matthews strode in. They'd been back at headquarters for a confab. Matthews grinned, "Damn Germans pulled out last night!" Kennefac sent Private Fisk out to the squads. "Tell 'em to saddle up and be ready to move."

An hour or so before dark we pulled out of Paestum. We had been engaged for a total of eight days; now the Germans were on the run.

Lieutenant Blumberg led the platoon across what had been no-man's-land. As it grew dark, we stopped on a dirt road between some fields and started to dig in for the night. It got too dark to see much. A few feet from where I stood was a large foxhole. I couldn't see the bottom, so I put my hands on the edge and vaulted down. My feet struck something in the chest-high hole—an M1 rifle,[6] a pack with a shovel, a full cartridge belt, and a gas mask. Some damn fool had gone off and left his stuff. I tossed it all out, curled up in the hole, and went to sleep.

When I awoke, the sun was already up. The stink in the air was overpowering—like squashed cats on a hot summer street. It wasn't cats; it was dead American soldiers. A few feet from my hole was another with the remains of a BAR team—two men blown into a faceless heap. The next hole had a heavy machine gun with two more decomposing corpses—one lying back in the other's arms—a dozen cartridge shells scattered at their feet. The next hole was empty except for a stripped machine gun. Fifty feet down the road was a battered jeep and a weapons carrier. Between them, balanced on his knees, elbows, and head, was a

---

6. The Garand M1 rifle, invented by John C. Garand, held a clip of eight bullets that fired as fast as one could pull the trigger.

GI who looked like he'd taken the full blast from a flamethrower. His entire front was scorched black, but his back was untouched. A wallet in his back pocket had an ID card—he was an artillery lieutenant.

Across the dirt road from my hole was a barn in a large field. In the field were four neat rows of GI helmets, packs, and gas masks. Apparently prisoners from the 36th Division had been lined up here before being marched off to captivity. Inside the barn was a cement floor littered with GI equipment partially burned on scattered hay.

At an intersection of our dirt road was a huge pile of rifles, packs, ammo, gas masks, and whatnot salvaged from surrounding fields. Either the Germans were moving too fast to take all this equipment or they may have planned to pick it up after wiping out the beachhead. Our eight-shot Garand MI rifles were superior to the German Mauser, yet they left them behind.

Sergeant Matthews was with me in the barn, and we went scouting into a grove of trees. Tank tracks in the dirt showed where the Germans had bivouacked. We followed the tracks out to a large field where men from the 36th Division had been overrun, squashed, shot, or bayoneted. They had been rotting there probably since the first or second day of the 36th's landing. What I saw corroborated what the two men from the 36th told me when they lost their unit and joined us.

It was about September 21 that we started the long chase north. The Germans led us on a long winding route through Eboli, Oliveto, Benevento, Pontelandolfo, Faicchio, Piedmonte, and Venafro. They slowed us down with rear-guard machine gun emplacements at strategic places. Their barrages took one or two men daily, and we got no replacements. After taking another hill one day, I said to Sergeant Kennefac, "We're getting nowhere fast. We knock 'em off one hill and they're sitting on the next one!"

Kennefac merely nodded his head and said, "That's how we're gonna win this war. We'll knock them off one hill after another until we get right into Berlin." He had better long-term vision than I did.

The army put us on our allies' right flank. I Company flanked the division, and my platoon flanked the company. I forgot the meaning of the word "rest." We did a lot of night attacking because we had become old-timers and trusted each other to be there in the dark. Night attacks cut down on casualties. We slept when we got the chance, but chances rarely lasted more than three or four hours. We had to keep abreast of the division to protect the flank, but we had to be mountain goats to keep up. If we hit a road for easier going, the eighty-eights drove us back into the mountains.

One day we had gallery seats as a regiment from the 34th Division attacked a mountain town across from us. It was like watching a movie as they swarmed up the slope and into town, but we were too far away to see individual fighting.

Another day, the mountains deserted us, and we hiked along a highway through a rolling plain. The Germans had zeroed in on an open hundred feet that we had to cross. I brought up the end of the platoon, and Lieutenant J. G. Evans was behind me. I ran like hell to beat an incoming shell and dived the last ten feet. Something just about split the back of my head. When I recovered from a momentary blackout, there was a heavy weight on my back.

The weight was Lieutenant Evans. "Did I hurt you, Doc? That damn shell was coming in!" When he dived, he landed on top of me, and his carbine rammed the back of my head. I staggered after the disappearing platoon. Eighty-eights got six men in rapid succession after that. Tech Sergeant Martinez was one of them. He had a dozen shell fragments from his feet to his fanny. One man from Martinez's platoon shot himself in the foot; he said it was an accident. Hell, my job was to patch 'em, not to judge 'em.

The platoon rejoined the company, and we trekked into the foothills where the eight-eights couldn't track us. We followed a winding river valley and came to a hill that our company commander wanted to attack. He insisted on a fifteen-minute artillery barrage before we charged. That might have been fine except that Moreno and Baca had scouted the hill the night before and reported there were no Germans on it.

During the attack we found ourselves opposed by two senile

old men, three old women, and four children. Their tree-sheltered home had miraculously escaped damage from our barrage, but the poor folks were scared out of their wits. Fortunately, the fellows weren't trigger-happy, and no one was hurt.

When the Germans reached the last bit of high ground south of Benevento, they set a beautiful trap and let us catch up to them. My platoon missed the trap because that day Lieutenant Blumberg took us to reconnoiter two mountain towns on our right flank.

On a long uphill climb, I fell behind to bring up a replacement who was too old and too fat for combat. I got fed up with urging him on and finally said, "We make fine sniper bait out here by ourselves." "Huh? What's that?" He was scared. "Why, hell! Those German snipers just wait for guys like us to fall behind so they can knock us off." *Whissht!* That guy went up the hill so fast I had to run to keep up.

Barely a half hour before we got to the first town, the Germans pulled out and machine-gunned the buildings as they went. All the walls were bullet pocked. Most of the civilians stayed indoors, but a few intrepid ones came out to greet us with bread and wine. We kept on through the town. An explosion far down the road turned out to be the Germans blowing up a bridge over a deep ravine. But blown bridges don't stop foot soldiers. Down we went and up the other side to the severed road. Artillery explosions roared in the town ahead of us. Fighting raged somewhere across the range to our left. Shells whooshed through the valley air at our level, and their explosions sounded far, far away.

Late that afternoon we reached our second town. This time the Germans had loitered and pulled out only five minutes before we arrived. Civilians turned out en masse to greet us, and Lieutenant Blumberg had a great time taking over the town in the name of the U.S. Army. The mayor, a very worried looking fellow, came out to greet us personally. His fat jowls flowed over his chin, and he wore a ridiculous cutaway coat. He escorted Blumberg to his offices in a two-story town hall that was also the schoolhouse.

There wasn't much of interest in this town. I did patch up a few civilians' minor wounds. One buxom eighteen-year-old lass took my hand and led me to the top of the stairs of the city hall–school. I wasn't sure what her intentions were until she lifted her dress and showed me several penetrating frag or bullet wounds to her inner thigh and tummy. I dressed the wounds and had to force her to swallow eight sulfa pills. There was no doctor in the town, and I didn't know how she would get the additional medical attention she needed. We were moving on, and I couldn't do more than give her the sulfa pills to combat infection.

Blumberg and Kennefac went to dinner at the mayor's house. They didn't rejoin the platoon until darkness settled over the town square. Small-arms fire in the valley below seemed magnified by the silence of nightfall. We started down into the valley to rejoin the company, but Blumberg led the platoon off the trail, and we had to send out scouts to reconnoiter. Matthews was furious; I kept to myself what I'd realized about Blumberg's eyesight.

Small-arms fire continued down in the valley; it grew louder as we approached and then stopped. Bob Shane, our weapons platoon mortar man, gave me a briefing. The company, on coming to the end of the meandering valley, had to cross a large fan-shaped field that rose in a gentle incline to a highway at its top. The Germans had machine guns all across the summit.

"Christ!" he said. "They could have wiped us out! Part of K Company and some of our fellows went out into the open, but instead of waiting for the whole battalion, one of their machine gunners got trigger-happy and opened up." The slaughter was avoided, and the men pulled back. "I got off thirty mortar rounds!" Shane was ecstatic. He loved nothing more than to fire his mortar. "The rest of I Company swung out to flank them and shot their asses out of there!"

The next morning we had to backtrack a quarter mile because three of our fighter planes were coming over to bomb. I hugged the ground between large boulders and bounced as wing bombs exploded on empty ground. I'll never know why the army bombed or shelled ground we already had.

Later in the day, word came by radio that our air corps had caught a convoy of five hundred German trucks and wiped it out. I looked at Matthews and said, "What do they expect us to believe next?" When we got to the high ground that the Germans had previously held, we saw it! Miles of smashed German trucks! News like this always made me think they were talking about somebody else. My division, the 45th, along with the 3rd and 34th Divisions, constituted the whole war in Europe at the time. The 36th Division had not yet recovered from Salerno. The news couldn't have been about somebody else.

We had finally knocked the Germans off their last bit of high ground. They backed up to the mountains beyond Benevento. We had been chasing them from Paestum in late September, and it was now early November 1943.

The road to Benevento was all downhill for us. We got a three-day rest on a scrubby hillside. It rained the first day, the first rainfall since we landed in Sicily. We weren't prepared with rain gear and were drenched. The rain brought out dormant cases of malaria. Within two days, we lost fifteen men in the company. The other two medics with I Company came down with high fevers, as did Sergeant Matthews and Lieutenant Barker. I got them all evacuated, against their will. Our company commander was also evacuated. He lay on the ground moaning and groaning, but I couldn't determine that he had a fever.

Within a few days we balanced our way across a catwalk leading into Benevento—all that remained of a once-massive bridge across the Volturno River. Benevento had been bombed before it was captured by the 34th Division. The broad main street was littered with rubble from bombed buildings. There were a couple of dead horses, bloated and swarming with flies. There was also something I couldn't figure out. It looked like a big ham in a vest—a body with no head, arms, or legs.

I Company led the regiment beyond Benevento and past the LOD (line of departure) into German-held territory. We passed grimy 34th Division riflemen going back to Benevento. One warned, "Watch out for tanks. They been running up close and firing point blank at us. Can't get anything to fight 'em 'cause of the blown bridge."

My platoon spearheaded the company, cautiously, with scouts out fifty yards on the point. It was about 10:00 in the morning as we advanced along a second-rate dirt road. Noon found us in open country with no cover whatever. The road had no gutters, and fields rolled away on either side. To our left the field sloped down to a gully full of pussy willows. Five hundred yards back we had passed the bend of a winding dry river—good cover. We stopped on the road, and all our officers went to the rear for a conference while we munched our rations.

A couple of hundred yards down the sloping road was a farmhouse in the field to our left. Across the road to the right of the farmhouse was a thicket. Sergeant Kennefac ambled over to me and kept looking at the clump of trees. He sat by me and opened a K ration. A shell whooshed through the air and exploded in the willows to our left. The next shell exploded in the field midway between the road and the willows down by the farmhouse. With no orders to move, we just sat there eating our rations. Pretty soon the farmhouse exploded into a mushroom of smoke. Someone down the road screamed.

Dusty Rhodes, our lead scout, came running up the road like the devil was behind him. Since he showed no intention of stopping, I yelled, "Grab him!" Charles Kroetsching, on the other side of the road, made a flying tackle but missed, and Rhodes raced into the field on our right. I grabbed my pouches and took off after him. It was a good fifty yards before I caught him and got him down so I could look at a two-inch back wound. Before I could bandage it, Rhodes pleaded, "Not here, Doc! They'll get us for sure!" He was up and away before I could stop him. I glanced back, and the whole company was racing through the field in a wild retreat. (I learned firsthand that one frightened man can panic an entire company.) I'll never know how a man with a hole in his chest could run like that. I finally caught Dusty, dressed his wound, and got him evacuated. I never saw him again.

When I headed back across the field, I found two more wounded men behind a haystack. Sam Shacter, an old-timer with I Company, was using their first-aid packets to care for them and doing a good job. One of the men was spitting blood. I ripped open his shirt and saw a nail-sized chest puncture. Lung wound! I sent Shacter back to find our aid station to evacuate the men.

While we waited, a couple of riflemen helped me dig slit trenches for the wounded. We were taking a few shells in the field, but not many. Then they stopped altogether. Sergeant Kennefac caught up to us, reorganized the platoon, and took it back to the road where we had been. He had picked up my pack from the road and dropped it at my feet.

We went down to the gully of pussy willows. It had water up to our thighs. Kennefac ordered all the men who had left their packs and rifles on the road to go up and get them. Though the men were nervous, no one argued with him. I never again saw our men leave their weapons behind.

Evans and Blumberg returned. They led the men out of the gully and up the slope to our left. The German tank picked us out and began shelling. Fortunately, the slope had furrows just deep enough to get us a bit underground. No one was hit, but as one shell exploded I stuck my head up to see the pack of a guy ahead of me disappear, though the fragment didn't scratch him. We took about ten shells, but by sheer luck no one was wounded.

We moved across the crest of our slope and were safe on the lee side of the shelling. Now, unmolested, we moved across the field parallel to the road we had left. By midafternoon we approached a farmhouse on a knoll about a hundred yards from a main road. As we approached, a woman and a young girl stood in the doorway. The woman pulled the girl inside and slammed the door. Moreno went forward and spouted Spanish. The door flew open, and the woman came out—she had thought we were Germans. She smiled happily. The house and everything in it was ours for the asking. Mamma slaughtered a small pig for us.

Lieutenant Blumberg sent a squad down to the main road, led by Louis Cordova. An artillery observer lieutenant and a man with a large radio joined us and set up in the barn, which had an open door to the kitchen. The lieutenant told us that the bridge to Benevento hadn't yet been repaired, but engineers floated some 105-mms, jeeps, and trucks across the river.

From a farmhouse window, we could see Cordova's squad at the road. Three German tanks came cautiously around a bend. When the first was practically on top of Cordova's men, a bazooka flashed and a dull explosion hit the tank's turret. It didn't seem to damage the tank, but I'm sure somebody inside was knocked cuckoo. Cordova's men were firing at the tank slits. The heavy-set man I'd brought up the mountainside a few days before panicked and ran from his safe cover. The German tank machine gunner almost decapitated him.

Blumberg called for the artillery lieutenant, who relayed fire orders. Our shells were far and wide of the tanks but close enough so that they slowly withdrew—first the last one, then the first two. I later learned that the artillery took credit for destroying three German tanks. I saw no hits. Louis Cordova received the Silver Star for his heroism.

The next day we swung around to our left in a large semicircle that brought us to the Volturno River again. At dawn of the following day, we made an unchallenged crossing. The water was only thigh deep, so I rolled my pants high to try to stay dry, then left them rolled up. The flashing whiteness of my legs drew Lieutenant Blumberg's attention. In the dawn light, and with his poor eyesight, he didn't recognize me. He came charging at me wondering what a British soldier was doing marching with his platoon. (The British wore shorts.) We both got a laugh out of that. Again, we were fortunate in our crossing—no opposition. Other regiments crossing at the same time had to fight their way across in the face of stiff German resistance.

At full daylight, we reached a large farmhouse surrounded by a vineyard. A leather-booted farmer stood watching us as we passed. He waved, "No tedeschi dieci kilometri!"[7]

At the very next bend in the road, the company ahead of us got machine-gunned from an overlooking hill. I was for going back to hang the farmer. Recalling the unnecessary shelling we had taken on the bare road out of Benevento, I went to the rear of the company to warn Lieutenant Evans of what lay ahead. Evans seemed irked with me. "What's the matter, Doc? Getting nervous?"

I was angry at his inference, and I told him what I thought

---

7. "No Germans for the next ten kilometers."

about being left in ass-open places without cover and no one to give us orders. Evans was a good man, and I should have kept my mouth shut. From that day on, I could see that he didn't like me.

The 1st Battalion ahead of us bypassed the German hill, so I Company took on the job. The Germans were sitting on more of a mountain than a hill and had good cover from numerous olive trees. The steep, irregular slope made getting at them perilous. We had to come down a barren slope, then attack upward. They had machine guns covering our slope, and we had no cover until we got down to the ravine.

A light rain began as we dropped our packs on the lee side of our hill. (Someone from supply would bring them to us later.) We prepared to attack in two groups of fifteen. A mortar man from the 1st Battalion was still there. He knew where the German machine gun emplacements were on their slope and volunteered to cover our attack with about twenty rounds that he still had.

Lieutenant Evans, who had come up to lead the first fifteen, was delighted. "Great!" he exclaimed. "You fire what you've got, and I'll see that you get more!" He and Kennefac and the first fifteen tensed for the mad dash. The mortar man began his one-man barrage, and away they went. I lined up with Blumberg and Matthews and the second fifteen, and off we went. Not carrying as much weight as the riflemen, I outran them and found myself in front with only an iodine swab for protection. I had to wait for them to pass me before I could continue. Meanwhile, the mortar man covered the Germans so well that they had their heads down and didn't see us coming. We were down and up and looking down on them before they knew what happened. We didn't have a single casualty. Soon firing rang out on the mountainside, but it was all ours.

I was on top behind a huge boulder with three riflemen when a Nazi officer, hands clasped over his head, seemed to be looking for us. A second German, carrying a burp gun, sneaked along behind him. The three riflemen fired simultaneously and blew them off the slope. A second Nazi officer came to surrender with hands overhead but kept edging over toward some bushes while Hogate called to him to stop. The German's head just seemed to flip as the three riflemen fired. From the clump of bushes the officer was edging toward, two Germans came running to surrender. Four more emerged. We now had six prisoners that I could see. They were a crummy looking lot.

Near me was a new medic we'd taken on after our other two came down with malaria. His name was Guy Pearce—and he was good. When the call "Medic!" came from above, I told Pearce to sit tight and I'd take it. I took off around a terrace and met Lieutenant Sturtevant, who had led the attack on this mountain from the other side. "Don't run, Doc," he said. "It's only a German. Ted Slifer shot him up there on the road."

Slifer (who looked like a riverboat gambler) stood behind a tree about twenty yards below a wounded German, who lay in the muddy mountain road. "Sorry to cause you trouble, Doc," he said. "Should've killed the sonofabitch."

I laughed at him and waved an okay. The German, a big fellow, lay on his back on the rain-soaked road. It looked as if he'd been running away and turned to fire at Slifer. Slifer's bullet took off his trigger finger and the tip of his nose and made such a big hole in his upper right arm that I could look inside and see the bone all chopped up. Big as he was, he was one sick cookie. I wasn't wearing an armband, so the German was apprehensive as I plopped down alongside him. I smiled at him. "Hi ya, you jerk!" He smiled back. I pulled out my hunting knife to cut away the sleeve of his heavy green overcoat. He sighed with relief when I started cutting his sleeve instead of his throat.

The Germans who had retreated from us and were on the opposite higher slope began shooting at me. A four-foot rock wall bordering the road caused them to shoot a bit high. Bullets spattered the mud only a foot beyond us. I guess to them it looked as if I was robbing a dead comrade. My patient looked worried about his buddies shooting at us. I didn't like it much, myself. "Some pals you got there," I said. Though he didn't understand English, I think he got my drift.

His arm wound was bleeding pretty badly. I put on a tourniquet, though there wasn't much clearance for it. I bandaged the hand with the missing trigger finger. The bandage on his nose looked funny. I couldn't go anywhere with bullets zipping all around me, so I stayed low alongside the German and went through his pockets. His wallet had several snapshots. One of a woman with two kids caused him to perk up. "Meine Frau und Kinder," he said. That wasn't hard to understand. Here was a guy with a wife and kids waiting for him back home. No different from our guys with families. I pulled out my wallet with pictures of my fiancée. What a stupid war . . . the Germans are trying to kill us and we're looking at pictures while bullets whiz around us. I took a couple of letters from him and stuck them in my pocket for s-2. Then, curious because most of our prisoners claimed to be Poles, Czechs, Austrians—anything but German—I pointed to him and said, "Deutsch?" His eyes lit up with pride, "Ja, Deutsch! Berlin!"

I got a little sadistic; I leaned on one elbow and cocked a thumb at myself, "Juden!" The German's whole body tensed. His eyes rolled wildly toward his rifle about two yards above his head, where Slifer's bullet had knocked it. I could see the terror in his eyes. I shook my head and smiled. His good arm reached over and patted my shoulder—"Gut! Gut!" he said.

Suddenly the skies opened up in a cloudburst with the largest raindrops I had ever seen in my life. The rain was so heavy I couldn't see through it. Neither could the Germans: they stopped shooting. I was drenched to the skin in two seconds flat.

I crawled away unseen. I came to Cowboy Wisecarver piling rocks around his light machine gun, preparing for a counterattack. We were both sopping. Cowboy said some officers on the dirt road below had some German shelter halves, so I went down to them. Two officers from s-2 were examining three camouflaged German shelter halves, as Cowboy had said. I walked right up to them and told them I needed the shelter halves for some wounded men. They gave them to me without hesitation, and I gave them the letters I had taken.

I went back to Cowboy and gave him one shelter half. I put one over myself, then crawled back to the German and put one over him. It was still raining buckets. Then I crawled away again—

Later I went to the aid station to replenish my medical supplies. The doctor turned to me with a vicious stare. "Where were you?" he said, as though accusing me of cowardice. It took me a few seconds to figure out what he meant. Then I shouted at him, "Who the hell do you think was holding that guy together while you sewed him?" Suddenly the doctor found other things to do and turned away.

That incident ended the calisthenics program. Because of the heavy rain and mud, we called that skirmish the Battle of Muddy Ridge, not to confuse it with Bloody Ridge in Sicily.

Three German machine guns atop a ridge held up the regiment as we neared Piedmonte. I Company had the job of knocking them off. Our captain came to me complaining of a fever and wanted me to evacuate him. His pulse was as steady as mine, and I told him he just had excitement fever and I wouldn't evacuate him. He went to the aid station anyway, and being an officer and a gentleman, our doctor evacuated him. That messed us up because the regiment had given him the plans for the attack, and he left without telling anyone what they were. Lieutenant Evans took command of the company. The men thought I was responsible for getting rid of our company commander and said I should get a medal. They didn't like him, either.

Instead of a frontal assault on the machine guns, we were guided by a friendly Italian farmer who knew of an unused trail up the hill that would flank the Germans. It was dark as we went up it. Our scouts captured the first two machine guns without firing a shot: the Germans were drunk and drowsing, two on each gun. A shot ahead of me killed the gunner on the third emplacement— he wasn't drunk. A motorcycle kicked over in the distance and sputtered away.

The wagon trail we were on turned into a substantial road that centuries of travel had worn ten feet deep. Ahead of me was an intersection through which a German machine gun sprayed flaming tracers. I paused to wait for a break in the firing before dashing across. Sergeant Kennefac came up, saw my problem, then calmly walked to the opposite side of the road and called to me. The road dropped off about three feet; I jumped down, safely down to a small mountain cabin where Sergeant Kennefac had set up our platoon CP. I told him about my wounded German, and he had two men take down a door between the cabin's main room and its one bedroom. We used that for a litter to haul the German down to the cabin. I put him in the only bed. I was shivering so badly that I told Kennefac, "If I don't dry out, I'm going to have pneumonia by morning."

Up to that time, we had never built fires other than small cooking fires. Now Kennefac said, "To hell with it!" The rain and clouds would mask smoke from the chimney. We broke up a couple of cabin chairs and built a roaring fire in the large fireplace. I stripped and stood naked, holding my clothes out to dry.

The next morning, when I brought the German a K ration breakfast, he turned so arrogant that I was sorry I'd saved his life. He wanted *real* eggs and *real* coffee. A couple of hours later, an ambulance came up the dirt mountain road and a very important driver and his assistant heroically carried my German patient away. What jackasses!

We bivouacked on that hill for three days. The rest of the battalion pulled into a tree-dotted area below us and spread out there. Artillery moved in with a 240-mm Long Tom and started shooting the damn thing. German planes zoomed low over us looking for it, but it had moved. They dropped their bombs in an empty gully.

Our company commander came back from his "malaria stint" in the hospital. "Men," he said, "you did a great job taking this hill. Tomorrow morning we'll start doing calisthenics to stay in shape." Where in heaven's name does the army get such military geniuses? We needed exercise like we needed more holes in our heads.

During our exercises, a German tank sneaked up on the hi overlooking us and laid in flat trajectory fire. Two men were kill and several were wounded. One boy I came across was almost (in half. His buddy was holding him together. I took over and s the buddy to the nearby aid station for the doctor. The doc came and sewed things together in the blood-filled body ca then sewed up the rest of him. Litter bearers hauled the boy a crawled past the intersection, and got back on the road where the embankments gave protection.

Lieutenant Blumberg took four men and went after a fourth German machine gun that we had bypassed at the ridge. It was holding up part of the regiment down below. The rest of us kept on moving down the walled road. I paused alongside a large cave dug into the right embankment. Sergeant Gregory came back from his platoon. "Didn't check this cave. Any of you guys check it?" No one had. Gregory stuck his rifle into the opening and yelled, "Come on out, you bastards!" I nearly fell over when four Germans came out with their hands in the air. Gregory didn't wait for more. He tossed in a hand grenade that exploded with a muffled roar. One rifleman took the Germans to the rear.

A couple of hundred feet more and we stopped. "All bazookas and grenade launchers forward!" German tanks were blocking the road to Piedmonte.

We spread out along both sides of the road. A German machine gun in the field to our right filled the night sky with tracers. A German machine gun in the field to our left also began to shower us, but the depth of the road was good protection. All was quiet, then someone came running toward me along our road at top speed, with five or six shadows racing behind him. A memory of the wild, disorganized retreat near Benevento flashed through my mind. When the lead runner got to me, I grabbed at his chest with both hands and almost knocked him backward. The guy was the same one whose ass Moreno had kicked and Hogate had been about to shoot above the meadow at Paestum. I shook him furiously. The other running men came to a halt around us. The guy I held whimpered, "Sergeant Cody said to retreat . . ." "Like hell!" I seethed. "Yes, he did," the coward whimpered. "He said to 'back up.'"

It was best to get rid of him. I gave him another good shake and said, "Go on! Get the hell out of here, but walk! Don't run!" The men who had been following him went quietly back to their squads.

The machine gun in the left field kept up a steady stream of tracers. Lieutenant Sturtevant came down the road and shouted, "They're shooting at you! Get the hell up there and shoot back!"

Four riflemen scrambled up the embankment, lay prone behind the rotted trunk of a fallen tree, and began blazing away toward the distant flaming machine gun. Three GIs had MIS with very little muzzle blast, but the fourth man, an eager new young kid had an '06 Springfield that threw a six-inch flame out the muzzle and another from the breech.

I had climbed the right embankment and was leaning against a tree trunk. Men began climbing my embankment, so I got down to make room for them. As I hit the road, the German machine gun picked up on the kid with the flaming '06 and raked him. He toppled off the embankment at my feet. Easiest casualty I ever got. But he was hit bad. I threw a blanket over him and crawled under it. I had a tiny two-inch-square flashlight that my fiancée had sent me. With it, I could see to bandage his trigger hand and splinted a leg broken just above his ankle. The worst wound was a hole down through his collarbone—just like the frightened kid on Bloody Ridge.

While I worked on the kid, Private Alcosure came to me and said through the blanket, "Doc, Blumberg's dead." Alcosure was a replacement who had been with us about a month, and he was a good, aggressive fighter. He was one of the men Blumberg had taken with him to knock off the German machine gun. "The bastards challenged us in English. We all went down, but Blumberg was puzzled and paused a second too long. They hit him in the face." "You sure he's dead?" "Yeah."

I didn't go to check it out.

Guy Pearce asked to look at one of his men. The fellow had been scouting the flank when he got hit in the eye; Pearce went out into the field and brought him in. His general condition seemed good—good pulse, no signs of shock. "Get something to cover him. Keep him warm." I went back to working on my own patient.

Our artillery cut loose with (I was told) a thousand-round barrage that lasted half an hour. All small-arms fire stopped. Someone called "Freeze!" The barrage had ended, and the silence

FIGURE 1. The confused jumble in the 45th Infantry Division landing area on Sicily. (Courtesy of 45th Infantry Division Museum)

FIGURE 2. Twenty-six-year-old Private Robert "Doc Joe" Franklin, during basic training at Camp Gordon Johnston in Livingston, Louisiana, 1942.

FIGURE 3. Willard Cody, First Sergeant of I Company, 157th Regiment. He was awarded the Silver Star, but his Legion of Merit (one of only sixteen awarded in the regiment) told it all. (Courtesy of Ardith Cody)

FIGURE 4. My fiancée, Betty Alliene Timmons—Timmy to her friends and me. At age four, she danced for Sid Grauman on the stage of Hollywood's famous Grauman's Chinese Theater. In what many call Hollywood's greatest silent western, *The Covered Wagon*, she sat on the seat of a wagon rolling west. Later, she performed ballet and tap dancing in films, became a high-fashion model, and changed careers to become an advertising executive at Bullock's department store in downtown Los Angeles. We met in the drama department of Los Angeles Junior College, where she was a star and I was a spear carrier. We became engaged when I was home on furlough shortly before I joined the 45th Division.

FIGURE 5. Charles Kroetsching. One day on Sicily, when he came charging through the underbrush thinking I'd been shot, I knew I had a true friend. I have never forgiven myself for not being with him when he was horribly, mortally wounded. I named my son after him so that he would never be forgotten—and my son has been a credit to his name.

Figure 6. This is what I looked like after five months of combat with I Company. First Sergeant Willard Cody saw that I needed a furlough—a three-day rest camp in Naples. He sent Charles Kroetsching along to look after me. My feet were so badly swollen from trench foot that, after four days in Naples, I was flown to a hospital in North Africa. This photo was taken by a street photographer in Naples, November 29, 1943.

FIGURE 7. The harbor at Anzio. Frequently, an Anzio Express shell exploding as troops were disembarking took a terrible toll. Stanley Clough, a fellow teacher at San Fernando Junior High School in Los Angeles, was with the Ranger unit that made the initial invasion landing at Anzio. He told me they captured the entire German garrison at a dance in town and advanced to within sight of Rome before the rapid German response drove them back. Clough was wounded and was being carried off Anzio as I arrived. (Courtesy of 45th Infantry Division Museum)

FIGURE 8. Fellow medic Guy Pearce. We had many dedicated medics throughout the war, but none more dedicated than Guy Pearce. His courage under fire and his devotion to the men of his platoon and company were incomparable. He was mortally wounded by artillery during the "Battle of the Underpass." According to my calculations, this happened on the second day; we had sent been out there the day before to help the 2nd Battalion when Pearce lost seven men in his platoon to a German eighty-eight shell.

FIGURE 9. First Sergeant Leon Shapley,
somewhere in garrison in the States. Medics
did not normally carry weapons in Europe
(although I did carry a .45 pistol when I got
to Germany). He was mortally wounded
in the canal where Richard Greszky is pic-
tured in figure 10. (Courtesy of Eric Jensen)

FIGURE 10. Aid station medic Richard
Greszky standing in the Anzio canal where
First Sergeant Leon Shapley was mortally
wounded. Many canals had waist-deep
water.

FIGURE 11. Nucleus of the 2nd Battalion aid station in France. From left to right: Myself, Robert A. Smith, Captain Irving Teitelbaum, MD, and Harold Smith.

FIGURE 12. Gordon MacPhail and another soldier, Herman Erde, with a little friend in Pertuis, France.

FIGURE 13. Great excitement in the southern French village of Pertuis, where we had our first weeklong rest after the invasion on August 15, 1944. We were the first American troops into Pertuis, and we were greeted with a hospitality that was repeated throughout France.

FIGURE 14. Captain Irving Teitelbaum, MD, holder of degrees from European and American universities. He spoke five languages, including fluent French. A true bon vivant and full of the joie de vivre, he was always smiling and bursting with good humor. He was a delight in our aid station until, about halfway between Pertuis and Rambervillers, he was killed when the Germans shelled our aid station. He was very much missed.

FIGURE 15. Michelle Joseph with her little sister and her brother. She was about eighteen or twenty and quite beautiful. Michelle—and dinner with her family— changed me from a hate-filled, vicious psychoneurotic back into a human being.

FIGURE 16. The aid station's mascot, Lena.

FIGURE 17. Lena with Gordon MacPhail, myself, and N. B. Terry, a quiet, thoughtful medic with the 2nd Battalion aid station and a full-blooded American Indian (I don't recall what tribe).

FIGURE 18. N. B. Terry and I with a group of French women and girls. Families greeted us joyously in every village and town we liberated.

FIGURE 19. When Gordon MacPhail and I were scouting locations for an aid station in the mountains above Grenoble in preparation for an attack the next day, we came across this orphanage. The parents of the children had all been slaughtered by the Nazis.

FIGURE 20. Gordon MacPhail with a young orphan from Grenoble. Fortunately for the 157th Regiment, the French Maquis (underground) liberated the city the night before we were to attack it.

FIGURE 21. Felix Sparks, superb combat commander in the 157th, rose through the ranks to become a brigadier general. He led the 3rd Battalion and I Company in the liberation of the Dachau concentration camp outside Munich. He was later a justice of the Colorado Supreme Court and commander of the Colorado Army National Guard.

(*Opposite*) FIGURE 22. Lieutenant General Alexander M. Patch, commanding general of the Seventh Army in Europe, presenting me with my second Silver Star. Patch is on the platform—I am in the mud.

FIGURE 23. Captain Arthur Murray, MD, came to us after the death of Captain Teitelbaum. I respected his medical skills, his professionalism, and his kindly attitude.

FIGURE 24. When rocket explosions became a bit too much, Captain Murray moved the aid station up to a medieval castle that overlooked the town of Bitche, France. It was large enough to accommodate all the villagers who came up to spend the night in safety. I am sitting on the snow-covered steps of the castle keep.

FIGURE 25. General Patton bypassed Aschaffenburg, Germany, and left some four thousand Nazi soldiers using this castle for a garrison. Because the Germans refused to surrender, we blew the town apart with artillery.

FIGURE 26. In five days of fighting, men from the 157th Infantry Regiment took Aschaffenburg house by house.

FIGURE 27. A group of German prisoners of war. The Germans always threw off their helmets and donned garrison caps when captured.

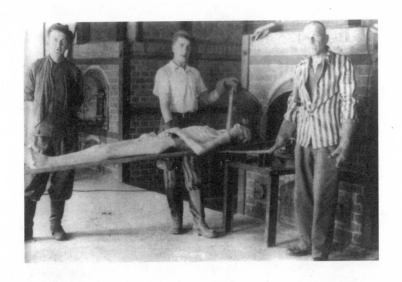

FIGURES 28, 29, 30. When the 3rd
Battalion and I Company, led by Lieutenant
Colonel Felix Sparks, liberated the Dachau
concentration camp on April 29, 1945,
the army and the world saw the horrors of
Hitler's solution to "the Jewish problem."
These three pictures (along with hundreds
of others), taken by Thunderbird Ed
Gorak, should convince any doubters that
the Holocaust was not a figment of the
imagination. (Courtesy of Edwin F. Gorak)

FIGURE 31. Our three beautiful
children: Charles, Patricia, and
Pam.

FIGURE 32. The 157th Infantry Regiment reunion in San Diego in 1990.
We don't look like much here, but we were a pretty ornery bunch of
hombres through two years of combat. From left to right: Felix Sparks,
the liberator of Dachau; Willard Cody, first sergeant of I Company and
recipient of the Silver Star and Legion of Merit; me, Robert "Doc Joe"
Franklin; Roger Hamann, a French volunteer who joined us in France,
was assigned to D Company and fought with us through the end of the
war; and Van T. Barfoot, a Choctaw Indian who rose through the ranks to
lieutenant colonel and received the Medal of Honor.

seemed worse than the shooting. Shadows came up the road and were right in the middle of us before we realized that we had eight fully equipped Germans. Whether they had come to surrender or were headed for the cave in the embankment, I don't know. They were dumbfounded when the riflemen surrounded them.

I confiscated a blanket from one of the Germans, spread it on the ground, and put my wounded kid on it. Willard Cody came by, and with his okay I placed four Germans on each side of the blanket to carry the boy back. My parting words to their guards were, "Shoot the first guy who drops his part of the blanket." That was a bluff, but if any of the Germans understood English, that may have convinced them they'd better be careful.

Through an interpreter, one of the German prisoners told us that our barrage had been wasted. The Germans had hightailed it to the far edge of the town and had a barrage of their own waiting for us. We waited until we were sure the Germans were gone before we entered Piedmonte.

In Piedmonte, in early November 1943, we had a weeklong rest. We were supposed to get "luxury" rations, but we didn't receive them, nor did we get our regular rations. So we had no food at all. A general came from somewhere to inspect us in bivouac. When our cook, Sergeant George Sichler, told the general we had no food, the general threatened to court-martial him for complaining. Again, I wondered where the army got such stupid generals.

When the Germans pulled out of Piedmonte, they took all the young girls with them. I learned this when, one evening, I went with Sichler to a farmhouse where a woman did his laundry. While there, the woman's husband came in. He told us he had complained to the Germans, so they took him too, as a prisoner. While we had wine and cheese around the kitchen table, he told us how he and others had been locked in a barn. "I killed the German guard with my bare hands and escaped to the mountains." He had just worked his way back home.

Sergeant Cody solved the food problem for one day. With company funds, he bought a cow that a farmer had hidden from the Germans. The cooks skinned and butchered it and hung it on a tree to "season" overnight. A guard with a tommy gun was placed to protect the carcass. The next day, all the officers in the regiment invited themselves to dinner.

Piedmonte was a small town with a stream running through it that turned the mill of a small textile factory. In one of the cobblestone streets an artist was copying pictures from postcards. For a pack of cigarettes, he painted a picture of Naples. I sent it to my fiancée, and I still have it.

It rained a lot. The weather turned freezing. We moved to the town of Venafro, at the base of towering mountains. We had come a long way from Paestum—Eboli, Oliveto, Benevento, Pontelandolfo, Faicchio, Piedmonte, and now what we called the Venafro Mountains—but were actually the towering Matese Mountains—part of the Apennine range.

4

Winter Line

On our first day in the Matese Mountains, we were late in arriving to take over positions occupied by our 1st Battalion. They couldn't leave their holes because the Germans were lobbing artillery shells into the lee side of the mountain. We moved along a road to the base of the mountain we were supposed to take over. We had a new officer, Lieutenant Robert A. Smith, who took Blumberg's place. He called a platoon meeting in a clearing a few yards above the road. I wasn't there; I'd gone farther up the mountain with Sergeant Hogate. He brewed coffee, and we split a can of cheese.

Venafro had been captured a few days before we moved into our position. Behind us stretched a beautiful valley loaded with vineyards, orchards, and about five hundred hunks of firepower ranging from ack-acks to 240s.[1] It was the coldest day I had experienced. Matthews, Fisk, Hogate, Staff Sergeant Emerson Voth, and I stood in a small circle stamping our feet and slapping our arms against our bodies. My teeth chattered so hard my jaw ached. Matthews laughed, "If you think this is cold, you ought to be back home in winter." (I think "back home" was a Kansas farm.) "My dad used to come into my room and pull the warm blankets off to get me up to help on the farm. I'd jump up and slam the window shut, then dive back under the covers to put on my clothes." He swung his arms some more and dug his hands

---

1. Ack-acks are antiaircraft guns.

into his jacket pockets. "Dad used to recite a little poem when it got cold like that":

> Cold blow the breezes
> Through the treezes.
> If'n it don't get warm,
> I'll freeze, b'jeezes!

Mathews chortled at the memory.

Now we were trying to relieve men on the mountain. It seemed peaceful enough while Hogate and I drank our coffee, but then the mountain shook with explosions that would have knocked me down if I hadn't been sitting. I ran down to the road but was stopped by a twenty-foot drop. A rifleman and Lieutenant Smith, holding a bleeding arm, staggered by. When they saw me they called "Doc! The CP!" and went on past.

I ran along the slope to where Lieutenant Smith had summoned the platoon. The first thing I saw froze me momentarily. Johnny Matthews had a jagged steel spike sticking out of his chest, and his mouth gaped like a fish out of water. He died within seconds. A couple of yards above him lay Mike Baca. Mike's left leg had been amputated at the thigh—not a drop of blood. He must have died instantly from the shock. A few yards farther up, against a rise, was another dead man. His face was so bloated it looked like he'd been slammed headfirst into the mountain wall and broken his neck. I didn't recognize him until I checked his dog tags— Sergeant "Cob" Kennefac!

There was no time to sit down and cry. Four other wounded men needed care. Our BAR man had a large hole in his upper arm. I patched him first. Two new arrivals were seriously hit. One's ankle was cut away, and he had numerous other wounds. His buddy, who had come to the company with him only a few days before, had the lower half of his face shot away.

While I worked, First Sergeant Cody arrived. He took one look at the dead men, turned pale, and walked away. Matthews and Kennefac were his particularly close buddies going back to their National Guard days.

First Sergeant Shapley drove up in the aid station jeep. He took care of my last wounded man and evacuated everyone.

I've never forgotten the boy without a jaw. His eyes looked terrified while I bandaged him. I smiled at him and said, "What are you so afraid of? You're going to be okay." The terror left, and he actually spoke: "Oo oo ink oh?" "Hell, yes! They'll fix you up fine in the hospital." Later I got a letter from Private Woody—the one with the shaved ankle—his buddy without the jaw was still alive, but in a bad way.

With former casualties and now this disaster, my platoon had only eleven men left out of forty. I walked up the road with Sergeant Cody as he called up the mountain, "Hogate, you're a staff sergeant . . . Voth, you're a sergeant." He made the promotions on the spot.

That evening we moved up to the top of the mountain. Hogate went down into a ravine to place what was left of the platoon. While he was gone, I found a shell crater that was big enough for a two-man slit trench after I pulled away enough loose sediment. I was making room for Hogate; I'd never before shared a slit trench.

At daybreak, our artillery shells began whooshing overhead. With the first one, I trembled from head to toe, my body like Jello. I didn't know what was wrong with me. I tried to control the shaking mentally, but I couldn't. Hogate woke up and said, "What's the matter, Doc? Cold?" "Guess so." I trembled as another shell went overhead.

Two walking wounded came to my hole. The wounds were minor, but I dressed them and sent the men back to our forward mountain aid station. That left nine men in the platoon. Nine out of the original forty.[2] I shook for three days and was totally useless. On the fourth day the trembling was gone and I was okay again.

During the nights following the deaths of Matthews and Kennefac, while I lay wet and cold in a shallow slit trench dug out

2. We had been losing men daily, mostly owing to artillery explosions, and we never got replacements.

of rock pulverized by a shell explosion, shuddering from head to foot with every passing shell, my brain functioning, but my nerves shot to hell, I became religious. I didn't believe in God. No benevolent God would ever allow what was happening. But I needed to appeal to some higher power to keep from going berserk. I prayed to my fiancée. I could only whisper, "Timmy,[3] help me . . . Help me . . ." (Now that she is gone after fifty-six and a half years of marriage, I regret that I never told her that she was God for me.) Something else happened during those nights—the words to "America the Beautiful" kept running through my head.

It rained all day and froze at night. I was always wet up to my chest. I had long ago thrown away my blanket, along with my gas mask. In a slit trench that filled with rain, there was no way to keep my bottom half dry. I wore my raincoat over my overcoat over my thin combat jacket over an OD shirt over long johns. We all discarded our blankets because once they got wet there was no way to dry them. We still wore canvas leggings, not realizing that when they got wet they tightened around our calves and cut off blood circulation. Unable to remove our shoes at night because we didn't know when the Germans on the opposite slope would attack, almost all of us developed severe trench foot (which one doctor told me was the advanced stages of frostbite). It got so bad that I couldn't feel my feet. But everybody else hobbled too, so it seemed okay.

Ted Slifer came down with appendicitis—his third attack since Sicily—but doctors in the hospitals wouldn't operate on him, though he was a great soldier and no slacker. Each time he had an attack he was in horrible pain. I had to evacuate him when he was desperately needed. I never saw him again.

Hogate was gone a good deal of the time. I was alone in our hole and became the command post, all by myself. Cody sent orders to and through me.

Bove, a former platoon member who had joined the newly

---

3. Timmy was a pet name for my fiancée, Betty Alliene Timmons. Everyone in our college drama department called her Timmy, as did I her whole life.

formed Scouts and Raiders after Sicily, came up one evening. "Doc," he called, "Cody said to check in with you. We're Scouts and Raiders coming through."

It was good seeing Bove again. He and half a dozen men vanished over the top of our mountain and machine-gunned the hell out of the German slope. I didn't see them again and assumed they took a different route back. I learned later that Bove had been killed on one of those raids. Eventually so many Scouts and Raiders were killed that the unit was disbanded.

After eight days, the company returned to our original bivouac at the base of the Venafro Mountains for a three-day rest. The peace was shattered when a battery of the 158th Artillery's 105-mms moved in only a few yards below us and started firing. I passed out cotton so the men could plug their ears.

Guy Pearce came to me with a very worried look. He was a great medic but always seemed worried. He was very conscientious about looking after his platoon. "Will you take a look at one of my men?" The man's feet were badly swollen and had turned black. I told Pearce to get litter bearers from our nearby aid station. To my knowledge, this was the first of hundreds of trench foot evacuations that followed in the weeks ahead.

I had one casualty in this rest area. A new boy with one of the other platoons shot himself in the foot. He said he was cleaning his rifle while eating and accidentally shot himself. It wasn't my job to tell him what a liar he was. I just got him evacuated. When I was in a North African hospital a month later, an I Company staff sergeant was in the next tent with this "accidental" shooter. He said to me, "Boy! This guy is a hell of a soldier. Told me how many Germans he killed before they shot him in the foot." I told the sergeant, "This guy was with the company for only two days. He never saw a German, and he shot himself in the foot in a rest area. But he's got a pretty good story if he convinced you, so don't tell anyone."

It was night when we left the rest area and climbed back into the mountains. I brought up the rear of my platoon, as usual, and the platoon brought up the rear of the company. That many feet ahead of me created a mudslide. My feet were so cold I couldn't feel the ground under them. For every step up, I slid back two or three. The platoon disappeared ahead of me, and I was desperate to keep up. Finally, when I fell I realized I could feel the ground with my knees. So I climbed that goddamn mountain on my hands and knees. When I got to the top, George Hogate was sitting on a boulder waiting for me. "Goddamn, Doc!" he laughed. "That's the best damn swearing I ever heard!"

I never swore before I got into the army. If I said "Hell!" my older brother reprimanded me with, "Why are you swearing?" In basic training, most of the hillbilly recruits couldn't think of the right words to express themselves, so every other word was a swearword. They thought I was strange because I spoke English. Now here was George Hogate lauding my swearing. I'd been cussing all the way up the mountain and didn't realize it. After that I swore to relieve my feelings, and I felt good about it.

My platoon of nine took over a mountaintop to the left of where we'd been before. I'll never forget the Mexican American staff sergeant who came across the barren flat exclaiming, "Jesus! Where did you get all the men?" We had nine—he had only six left.

On the opposite slope, Germans openly lounged about, unconcerned. The sergeant said, "For chrissake, don't shoot at those guys. They've got this whole spot zeroed in with mortars. They'll blow hell out of you!" We took the sergeant's word for it and didn't shoot at them.

Hogate and I rigged a shelter half over two huge boulders to keep out the rain. It worked fine if you didn't touch the material. Wherever you touched it, water poured in.

We got three new men. Two came back from the hospital, and a new lieutenant named Yentis replaced Lieutenant Smith. He looked a little out of shape for combat, but he turned out to be a good man. Now we had twelve men in the platoon, counting the lieutenant and me.

On the opposite German slope there was a cave. Every once in a while the Germans would roll out an eighty-eight, fire it, and roll it back into the cave. We sent to Cody for an artillery observer.

The guy came out and said, "Damn! We've been looking for that gun!" He called in artillery on it, but they never hit the cave.

On the morning after Yentis arrived, he came up to Hogate and me and said, "Those two men who came up with me were sleeping when I checked the ravine. What should I do about them?" Hogate didn't answer. He just picked up his M1 and said, "Better clean my rifle. Want one, Doc?" "Yeah," I answered. "Better have one." I got a rifle from a pile of abandoned ones. I had no intention of ever being captured. Yentis wisely took Hogate's response as "Don't do anything," and went back down into the ravine.

Every morning after that the Germans attacked. Fortunately for us, they attacked the hill on our left. Had they hit us, we didn't have enough men to hold them. Paratroopers covered that hill with automatic weapons. When the Germans hit the barbed wire we had strung in the ravine and went through, the paratroopers blew them away. It sounded like a real war.

One night while Hogate was checking his men in the ravine, Sergeant Voth came up to me with two Germans. "Treat them good, Doc," he said. "They came up behind me in the dark and could have killed me. One said in English, 'We are two German soldiers. We have come to surrender. We have one pistol.'" I told Voth to take them back to Cody in the company CP.

The next day Private Henry Fisk "swam" through the mud to tell me, "Pack your gear, Doc. You're going to Naples for a three-day rest."

I told Fisk I couldn't leave when we had so few men, but he said men were coming up to replace me and Charles Kroetsching, who was also going. I thought that as long as someone was replacing us, it was okay to go. At the time, I didn't stop to reason why. It took a long, long time before I began to realize that Hogate had told Cody about my uncontrollable trembling. Cody had to get in touch with our aid station doctor to get a medic replacement for me, and he sent along Charles Kroetsching, my close buddy, to look after me, though at the time I didn't realize I was being "looked after." So my rest trip to Naples wasn't just freak good luck.

While Kroetsching and I prepared to leave, Lieutenant Yentis asked if I had any money. I told him no, and he gave me a hundred Italian lira. The army had devalued the lira to two cents American, so I had two dollars for my trip.

Kroetsching and I were in the company CP with Cody when a runner brought word that a German patrol was moving in the ravine at the base of our mountain. Kroetsching said, "If they fire one shot, I'm going back to my hole!" If he went back, I was going back too. Fortunately the German patrol went past, and no shots were fired.

That morning was the only time I saw Cody explode with anger. "Look," he said to me. "I ordered overshoes for the company, and they sent me six pairs!"

Cody asked me what he should do about the men's trench foot. I told him I had a tube of boric acid ointment that I rubbed into my feet. If Gertrude Ederly smeared her body with grease to combat the cold when she swam the English Channel, I figured the greasy ointment might help. Cody later told me he had ordered boric acid ointment from the aid station for all the men, and that my suggestion had saved the company.

Sterling Johnson, the clerk who had risked his life to bring us mail at Paestum, knew the trail back and was going to lead us. However, we were asked to sidetrack to L Company to carry back a wounded man. When we got there, it was dark. A medic with L Company, a man named Long, assured his patient (who had a bad buttock wound) that I was a good medic and would take good care of him. Long had been with the 3rd Battalion aid station in Sicily and was one of the men who hated me for setting the example of working under fire. Now that he had been with a company a few months and had his men's respect, he apologized for the way he had acted. He now knew what it was to be a "line medic."

Being sidetracked to L Company caused Sterling to lose the trail back. We got lost in the pitch-black night, and I mean pitch. I couldn't see a foot in front of me. There were now eight of us all together, with some men from L Company. We took turns hauling the litter, but we couldn't see where we were going. I scraped my frozen feet along the ground to feel my way. When it was my turn to carry the litter, I was in acute pain. I wasn't strong enough to do the job, but I tried. Once I slipped yet managed to hold on to the litter. But I twisted under it to keep it from dumping the wounded boy and threw out my back.

Once a man up front called, "Halt!" His shuffling feet had hit empty space. He threw a rock and didn't hear it land. We were on the verge of falling over a cliff. We backed up. All of us were having trouble with trench foot, and we were making no progress. I talked to the staff sergeant from L Company. "Leave me here with the litter and get litter bearers from our aid station. We'll never get back this way." It was so damn dark that I couldn't even see him, though I felt he was right in front of me.

The boy on the litter heard me and cried, "If you leave me, I'll get up and walk!" Of course he couldn't. The staff sergeant said, "Goddamnit! We're going to take him with us! We're men, not women!" I was glad to be informed of the fact.

I called to Charles Kroetsching. I couldn't see him, but he came to me. I told him I was going to take off to find the aid station and send back a litter squad. It was so dark that I disappeared in one step. I didn't know where in the hell I was, or where the aid station was, but I shuffled and stumbled and fell and shuffled some more. Somehow I seemed to recognize certain mountain peaks against the skyline. Lost or not, I always seemed to find my way to where I was going. I finally found the trail we had taken coming back into the mountains from our rest area. It was all uphill, and I could see the skyline above me. As I neared the top, a voice called, "Halt! What's the password?"

Oh, goddamnit to hell! I had come all this way and some bastard was going to shoot me! I yelled, "I'm a medic with I Company. We don't have passwords on the front lines!" I cut loose with all the swearwords I had learned and a few new ones. The sentry, standing behind a tree, said, "Pass, friend."

Swearing did have some use, after all.

The sentry showed me the way to a small mountain village and our forward aid station. When I opened the door to the cabin, I stood transfixed. There was a roaring fire in a large fireplace.

Medics lounged around tables. Dr. Sternlieb was there. Our regimental commander, Colonel James, sat at one end of the room with his elbows on a table. He was an officer from the 45th National Guard days and a very pleasant gentleman. When he asked me how things were at the front, I told him about our nine-man platoon and the German attacks against the hill on our left. He merely looked thoughtful, nodded, and said nothing.

The aid station personnel were very kind to me. When the doctor summoned a litter squad to go after the wounded L Company man, I started to go with them. Sternlieb said it wasn't necessary for me to go. I told him I'd take the squad to the head of the trail and get them pointed in the right direction, and I did.

Again the medics were kind to me when I returned to the warm cabin. One gave me a pair of dry socks. Another gave me his soft bed in the next room, and I slept until daybreak. Then I had a cup of coffee and was relieved to notice that the L Company patient had been brought in and was on a litter on the floor. I headed for the trail down into the valley where we were to get trucks to take us to Naples. It was Thanksgiving Day 1943.

Charles Kroetsching was waiting for me at the top of the trail. "Where were you, Doc? I saved you a place in a hay barn." Sterling Johnson was also there and thanked me for sending the litter squad. As we started down, Cowboy Wisecarver was coming up with a three-mule train. Each mule carried six artillery shells—three in cases on each side. Cowboy carried a three-pack of shells while pulling the mules. What a man!

When we got down to the valley floor, we were informed that the trucks that would take us to Naples would be a day late. Our I Company kitchen truck was there—badly shot up. They'd been hit by a German barrage the day before. Our chief cook, George Sichler, had been wounded and evacuated. All the pots and pans were full of holes. Instead of a hot turkey dinner for Thanksgiving, the cooks were making cold turkey sandwiches to send into the mountains.

One cook told me what happened the day before. A big, friendly white dog had appeared out of nowhere. It circled the kitchen truck, letting everyone pet it. Then it pranced around each of the 158th's artillery pieces and vanished as suddenly as it had appeared. Within a few minutes, the German barrage blasted the entire area. German observers high on the mountain had watched the dog as it spotted the targets by circling them.

The trucks arrived and took us to Naples. We had a clear view all the way down the valley. Mount Vesuvius was blowing smoke. In a rest camp that had been an Italian garrison, I got a shower, a change of clothing, and a pair of shoes many sizes too large so I could squeeze my swollen feet into them.

Kroetsching and I just wandered around sightseeing. A street photographer took my picture in front of a lion on a pedestal. Naples was a shambles. It had been bombed from the air, and some sort of time bomb blew up the main post office, killing a lot of people.

On our second evening, Charles and I were window-shopping in a crowded street as it grew dark. Suddenly, sirens wailed a warning of bombers. Shoppers were pushed out of shops, and owners buttoned everything up. The streets emptied, and the two of us were standing all alone. I could hear the bombers overhead, but that was no concern. Hundreds of thousands of tracers filled the night sky as arc lights made paths for the bullets. I couldn't see the bombers in the arc lights—they were "too bloody 'igh"—but I could hear the bombs exploding near the harbor.

On our third day we took an army "tourist" truck to Pompeii. My feet hurt so badly that I had trouble hobbling on the narrow cobblestone streets of the ancient excavated city. Down one street was a whorehouse nearly two thousand years old. A massive plaster penis jutted into the street from above the entrance. A red rag was hung from it when the place was open for business. (Probably the origin of "red light district.") Several "cribs" on either side of the entrance were made of hardened lava. The main (waiting?) room had murals all around the ceiling. They showed every sexual combination—men with women, men with men, women with women, men with animals—whatever one could imagine. Along one wall in the street were two covered panels. For a couple of lira, a guard-attendant uncovered them. One showed a god with two huge penises—one for all day and one for all night.

The other panel showed a character with a huge penis weighed on a scale balanced with a pile of gold (I guess it meant it was worth its weight in gold).

The main, and only, completely restored house at the time was a beautiful structure. At the entrance was something I had seen in my high school Latin book—a mosaic of a snarling dog with the warning *Cave Canem!* Beware of the Dog! Inside, at a small sales counter, I bought two color photos of the panels around one of the rooms. I still have them; they're a rarity.

Our three-day furlough was extended to five, so we had two more days to wander. I stopped in at a bakery that displayed delicious-looking pastry. I bought half a dozen pieces. Outside, I took a big bite of one, then spit it out. No sugar! I gave all the pastry to a passing child.

That night I awoke screaming. My trenchfoot was "thawing," and the pain was unbearable. Fortunately Charles Kroetsching, who had been shacking up with some young girl,[4] was asleep in the cot next to mine. I sent him down to the infirmary for codeine and aspirin, but they didn't help. My feet were so tender that I couldn't let the sheet touch them. In the morning a couple of fellows with a litter hauled me off to a local hospital. At first I refused to go, since I didn't want to leave my platoon in the lurch. But Charles said, "Can you walk?" I couldn't, so I let them take me away after telling Charles to have Sterling Johnson hold my mail.

I sat on the edge of my cot in the bombed-out building that was the hospital. I was in agony and asked a nurse to bring me a large pan of cool water. Sitting there with my feet in the water worked miracles to alleviate the pain. I fell asleep sitting on the edge of my cot. The nurse came by, and I woke up. She said, "Now I've seen everything!"

Later that day I was transported to an airfield and carried

---

4. In Naples during the war, it seemed to be common for mothers to sell GIs spaghetti in the kitchen and their daughters in the bedroom. The girls were all supposedly sixteen or older. I never participated in these relations myself because I had my beautiful fiancée waiting for me back home (if I ever got home). Charles, however, was free to indulge.

onto a C-47.[5] My litter was over one wing. As we flew across the Mediterranean at an altitude of a couple of hundred feet to avoid German fighter planes, I watched in fascination as the wing flopped up and down like a bird's.

I spent the next two months in a North African field hospital— December 1943 and all of January 1944. The first hospital I was sent to did nothing for our feet. I don't recall that any doctor ever even looked at us. In our tent we rubbed boric acid into our feet and joked a lot to cover our pain. In the first few days a pretty nurse walked into our tent opening, looked at us with a sneer and said, "You're all a bunch of fakers!" Instead of getting understanding or compassion, we were insulted. In the tent next to ours, I was told, feet were being amputated because gangrene had set in. In another tent the trench foot patients were getting some kind of spinal shots to try to open up veins so blood could circulate to the feet. I think we were lucky to be left alone to massage our feet. In February the hospital moved, and we were sent to a replacement pool to get us ready to go back to the front. I couldn't walk yet. At the replacement center we were ordered to go on five-mile hikes. I went, but I hobbled in a couple of hours after everyone else. A lieutenant who met me on my return called me a "fuck off" and informed me that he knew what it was like at the front.

I heard that Sam Shacter was in one of the tents. I went to visit him and found him in tears of frustration. He told me that a sergeant had berated him because he was in bed and hadn't gone on the hike. A shell had blown off half of Sam's hand and broken his leg, which wasn't yet healed. The sergeant threatened to court-martial him.

I volunteered to get out of there and return to my outfit. There was no problem, but first I had to see a "psychiatrist" who would approve my return. I was in line with others waiting to see him, and fellows were coming out of the tent in tears. When I went in I could see why. The "psychiatrist" sat at a small table and didn't look up to see who I was. He doodled on a pad and asked,

5. The C-47 was a cargo plane that was also used to drop paratroopers.

"How's your sex life? Getting any?" I've met jackasses in the army, but this character took the cake.

Returning to my outfit was probably one of the most frightening experiences of the war. We were put in the bottom of an empty liberty ship, and the ladder was pulled up. Had we been torpedoed, we would have drowned like rats. The walls of the ship were so thin that it sounded as if the waves would burst through. I was thankful when we finally landed at Naples. There I heard my division had just landed at Anzio, wherever that was, and was losing a thousand men a week. Of course that was an exaggeration, and many of the returnees went to the local hospital to complain about their feet and try to get reclassified. I just wanted to get back to my outfit.

5

Anzio to Rome

Anzio is thirty-seven miles south of Rome. The landing there was supposed to draw German forces away from Monte Cassino and aid forces attacking it. It didn't work. Instead, the Germans brought down heavy reinforcements from north of Rome, and within a week our troops were outnumbered. They took the high ground all around Anzio, something our "brilliant" commanders failed to do, and locked us in for four months.

The arrival at Anzio was nightmarish. About a hundred of us disembarked and straggled through deserted, war-torn, bombed streets. Cut telephone wires hung from toppled poles. From dugouts in the rubble, ack-ack guns pointed skyward, and their silent, solemn-eyed crews watched us as we dodged through the street.

A few hundred yards out of town we waited for trucks to take us to our units. From where I stood, I had a good view of the Tyrrhenian Sea. Six cruisers and destroyers sailed single file and discharged a heavy smokescreen, circled back into it and let loose a thunderous bombardment shoreward. Lieutenant Sturtevant, who had been with a group of officers, came over and greeted me warmly. I hadn't known that he was on the LCI that brought us to Anzio.

Instead of going directly to I Company, I stayed for a few days at our 3rd Battalion aid station. Sergeant Shapley had saved a pair of rubber overshoes for me, since it rained a lot. The first night our regiment's Catholic chaplain, Father Raley, came into the tent looking for someone to help him get a bale of hay for

British soldiers who would be coming in that night. He thought it would be a nice gesture to spread it on the wet ground so they'd have a dry spot to sleep. No one there volunteered, so I did. The bale was a few hundred yards out in a field, and the damn thing was too heavy to carry, so we rolled it over the wet ground. The chaplain prayed and I swore, and we finally got it to the aid station area. Raley took it from there.

The next morning I took the trail through heavy brush to our kitchen truck for breakfast. On the side of the trail were four British soldiers under blankets, lying on the hay that Chaplain Raley and I had brought. Only their heads showed as their eyes followed me. "Hey," I said. "Come have breakfast with us." Their eyes lit up. "Breakfast with you Americans! Sure thing!" They threw off their blankets and had happy faces as they joined us. It made me feel good to have invited them.

On the third day, Lieutenant Sturtevant came to me. "The men want to know when you're coming back." I asked him to wait for me to gather my gear, and I went back with him. I Company was bivouacked a short distance behind a British unit and was barely hidden by scrawny brush. It was almost at full strength, with about two hundred men, having had replacements since our nightmare in the Venafro Mountains.

Kroetsching was in a hospital, probably in Naples. The sweet young thing he had shacked up with in Naples gave him a sweet dose of the clap. I was glad he was out of it for a while. Martinez was now my platoon tech sergeant. Voth was a staff sergeant. I didn't see Hogate, and it wasn't until after the war when I asked Cody what happened to him that I was simply told, "He got killed." I never asked where or when.

Baide Black, who had become the regimental major's radio-man, was killed early that week when the two went up front for a look-see and an eighty-eight got them. Louis Cordova was also killed early that week when a new lieutenant set up a couple of machine guns and didn't clear his men out of the field of fire. Our own machine gun killed Louis.

Mitchell and Pearce, 1st and 2nd Platoon medics, were still there. I brought out replacements for them, but they refused to leave their platoons for a rest. Mitchell had developed a bad tic; his cheek twitched, and his eye fluttered nervously. He had also developed a stutter. Still, he refused to leave his men. Pearce seemed okay; he was as quiet as ever.

First Sergeant Willard Cody, Lieutenant Yentis, and J. G. Evans, now a captain, were still there. Several of the old-timers were still in the hospital with trench foot or wounds. I didn't see Ted Slifer, Bombard, Richardson, Moreno, Bennett, or Charpentier. Our former chief cook Staff Sergeant George Sichler, Cowboy Wisecarver, Tech Sergeant Johnny Cohen, Tech Sergeant Youtsey, Lieutenant Cook, Tech Sergeant Kenneth Kindig, Henry Fisk, Sterling Johnson, Louis Stamas, and a few others were still there. I didn't know any of the new men. I never even knew their names before they got killed.

The first day after my arrival, the platoon met with our new lieutenant, whose name I never knew. Someone brought in Louis Cordova's rifle that had a scope on it and asked the lieutenant who to give it to. The lieutenant said, "I'll take it." Tech Sergeant Martinez, angry because the lieutenant had caused Cordova's death, growled, "Lieutenant, if you want that scope, you're going to have to get up there where you can use it!" The lieutenant was flustered, but Martinez intimidated him. Martinez gave the scope to one of the fellows there.

The day after my arrival, February 16, 1944, two platoons and our machine gun section were led through a maze of accordion barbed wire strung in front of us by the British and headed out across open country. Word was that we were going to help our 2nd Battalion, which was in trouble. German artillery zeroed in on us. From their positions on the high ground around Anzio, their observers could see our every move. We dodged through the explosions but lost one man to a German fighter plane that screamed low over us and dropped a bomb. I checked his body but found no wounds. The concussion must have killed him.

One new man found a nice hole to duck into from the shelling and didn't want to get out of it. I told him he'd get killed if he stayed there, and I kicked his ass so hard that I scared him more than the eighty-eights did.

We lost seven men in Pearce's platoon when they jumped into the nice safe ditch bordering the Albano-Anzio highway we'd been heading for. An eighty-eight round landed in the ditch just as the men did. I arrived only seconds later. Pearce was desperately trying to hold three wounded men on the slippery wall of the ditch, which was thigh deep in water. Pearce called to me, "There are two men underwater!" I fished around under the muddy water and pulled them both up, but they were dead. I tended two men who had lesser wounds and helped Pearce with the three men he was trying to keep from slipping under the water. We rendered first aid as best we could. Fortunately a British high-top ambulance came from the direction of our 2nd Battalion and took all of our casualties. Pearce and I waded up the ditch toward the rest of our platoons.

The Albano-Anzio highway was just a macadam road that ran from Anzio toward Rome, but it was the strategic main supply road. About fifty yards down the road, in back of us, was a bridge over a twenty-foot-high railroad embankment. The army called that opening the Overpass. The British called it the Flyover. Those of us who fought there called it the Underpass.

I had trouble walking because my overshoes filled with water, so I took them off and threw them away. Across the road from me, about a couple of hundred feet away in a field, was a farmhouse. Behind it was an American tank. On the road between me and the farmhouse was an American fighter plane that had been downed. An officer from the tank was reaching up to pull something from the plane when a Messerschmitt screamed over the Underpass and up the road with his machine guns wide open. Bullets broke both forearms of the scavenging lieutenant. I had only a few feet to go to take care of him. I splinted both arms and slung them in triangle bandages.

We stopped in the ditch while our scouts went forward to contact 2nd Battalion and check on the situation. The battalion was in an area known as "the Caves" and was in the path of a tremendous German effort to wipe out the beachhead.

When I started to dig a hole in the side of the ditch I exposed the tail of an unexploded bomb, so I very quickly moved about twenty feet upstream and dug my trench. An eighty-eight hit the wall of the ditch directly across from me. It buried itself in the soft dirt before going off, but the explosion was so close I could hear the steel casing rip. That's close! My helmet protected me from the shower of mud and rocks that rained down on my head. I glanced up the ditch; Sergeant Voth was looking at me, and his mouth was flapping. "Poor guy," I thought. "He's gone nuts!" It took me a while to realize that I was deaf. My ears rang for a while, but the deafness wore off.

Our scouts came back from 2nd Battalion; they'd been told we weren't needed. Eight casualties and not needed. We waited for nightfall to return to our former bivouac area. Tech Sergeant Martinez and I doubled up with one shelter half under us and one over us to ward off the light rain. We didn't dig slit trenches. I guess it was sometime after midnight when I was awakened by "firecrackers" going off east of us. I shook Martinez awake. "What is it?" I asked. "Personnel bombs," he muttered and went back to sleep. I shook him awake again. "Ours or theirs?"

"Theirs," he mumbled. Martinez was an old-timer, and I was new to the beach, and if he didn't seem concerned, why should I be? However, I hadn't quite gotten back to sleep when I heard the offbeat whir of German bombers overhead. Motors of German bombers weren't synchronized. That's what caused the whir-whir. Our bomber motors were synchronized and made only a single whir through the night. The German bombers dropped chandelier flares that lit us up like daylight and seemed never to go out. They circled over us and dropped long canisters that split open and whirled out foot-long personnel bombs with a propeller in the nose and noisemakers in the tail. I don't know how many bombs were clustered in each canister, but there were a lot of them. They came screaming down and raised hell with us. Martinez and I were as exposed as nudes in an art class, but we never got a scratch. Men all around us were hit in their holes. Obvious wounds I could bandage, but I didn't know what to do for guys bleeding from their mouths, ears, and noses. I got the walking wounded to our nearby aid station and was still working at daybreak. I evacuated Martinez. The inoperable steel he carried in his legs almost crippled him in the cold, though he never complained. I told him, "Martinez, you're too damn slow. You're going to get killed." He didn't argue. It was the last I saw of him.

I was bandaging a British soldier who didn't have a lower half to his face when Willard Cody led the company past me. He called, "Stay with the wounded! I'll send someone back for you!"

Lieutenant Cook of I Company's weapons platoon had a slit trench near our aid station. He had placed metal rods over it but hadn't covered the rods. He got a direct hit. We got him into the aid station, but he was in deep shock, and the doctor couldn't get plasma into him. Suddenly he came out of a coma and seemed quite lucid. He asked to talk to Louis Stamas, so someone got Stamas, and they talked. I thought Cook was going to be okay, but he died within minutes after talking with Stamas.

Later that morning I ran to the sound of a loud explosion. Lieutenant Lehman, an "explosives expert," had found a butterfly bomb that hadn't exploded. He sat cross-legged on the ground with three men around him trying to figure out what was wrong with it, and he must have given the propeller a couple of turns. When I got there Lehman had no arms or legs, his head was flat as a pancake, and his brains lay in a neat pile about a yard away—as if someone had scooped them out and laid them there. The men around him were dead. I treated a wounded man about thirty yards away on a dirt path.

Cody had left our mortar section behind, so I went to stay with Bob Shane. Stamas came to get me early the next morning. We were guided through the British accordion barbed wire and went right back out to where we had gone to help the 2nd Battalion, only we took a road to the Underpass, then went under that and out to Cody by the farmhouse. The tank was still there, and there was another one bogged down in the mud about ten yards in front of the embankment and thirty yards left of the Underpass opening.

The company had just survived a fearsome German artillery barrage and repulsed waves of attacking German infantry. Cody immediately sent me to the farmhouse, which had a lean-to shed, open on both sides, with a lattice rear wall. The roof was made of tiles. On open ground on my way to the shed were three dead men. One, lying on his back with his arms bent upward from his elbows, was my good friend Henry Fisk, who had just turned twenty in Sicily.

Lying on the ground in the shed were about ten seriously wounded men. The worst hurt was Guy Pearce. He had taken a direct hit from an eighty-eight in the right front of the farmhouse where Fisk lay dead. The other wounded there had been hit at the same time. An officer from the tank behind the farmhouse told me Pearce, hit as badly as he was, was crawling around trying to aid the others. He and some of his tank men took over, and Pearce was telling him how to treat everyone. The tank men had carried everyone into the shed. I asked the tank lieutenant to write Pearce up for a Silver Star, and he responded as though he should have thought of it himself: "I will!" And he did. I regretted that I hadn't asked for a DSC or a Congressional Medal of Honor. At the time, to my knowledge, medics could not get above the Silver Star. In my division, the higher medals were reserved for "killers."

I spent the day checking wounds and bandages. The tank men generously gave me all the blankets on the tank so that I could cover the wounded, and I asked the lieutenant to radio for medical supplies and plasma. There was no response. Pearce was so seriously wounded that it was amazing he was alive and conscious—broken right leg, multiple penetrating and perforating wounds of both arms, abdomen, chest, head, and face. As I worked over him he swore a blue streak at me. Then he apologized . . . "Sorry, Joe . . . it hurts."

In the late afternoon, a couple of Germans crawled down the ditch and set up a machine gun under a British ambulance that had been toppled into the ditch by an eighty-eight. They were firing down our flank in front of the farmhouse. Five riflemen came running into my makeshift hospital. One said, "Cody sent us to protect the wounded!" I told him to get the hell outside and protect them. He wasn't doing any good in there. They immediately went out the far side of the shed and must have thrown grenades under the ambulance, because it burst into flames and the machine gun went silent. That fire burned all through the night.

I Company wasn't alone. There were several British with us who had been cut off from their unit by a German penetration of the left flank. There was also a platoon from L Company in front of the farmhouse. M Company had sent a 20-mm machine gun that was placed in the left embankment of the Underpass. An eighty-eight made a direct hit on them that killed two gunners and bent the gun's barrel. While I was in my "hospital," a pioneer platoon from headquarters brought in supplies and ammunition and a new barrel for the 20-mm gun. New M Company men took over the gun.

A frightened soldier from L Company came into the shed to hide and curled up to rest in a corner where I kept my gear. I kept having to kick him out of my corner. Through an opening in the farmhouse, I could see out into the battlefield and was worried about GIs who stood up from their slit trenches to get off a good shot. They exposed too much of themselves.

At dark I was dozing in my corner when Cody shook me awake and said we were going to get the wounded out. I was greatly relieved, but I didn't know how we were going to do that. Our jeep and trailer were in back of the Underpass with food, ammunition, and litters. Riflemen carried the wounded back. There was an ambulance there with litter bearers, but they refused to come onto the battlefield: "We got orders to just load the wounded when you guys bring 'em back here." I was so disgusted I swore at them and told them to get the hell out of there. We could load the wounded ourselves. They seemed relieved to get out of their "dangerous assignment" and disappeared into the night.

We loaded the ambulance, placed four walking wounded in the back of the jeep, and put two litters on the trailer. Pearce was on one of them. There were six wounded on litters that we laid on the ground alongside a tank on the right of the Underpass opening. We'd have to come back for them. I stood on the trailer hitch with one hand grabbing the back of the jeep and the other grasping two adjacent stretcher handles. I went back for two reasons: I wanted to make sure Pearce was looked after, and I was out of medical supplies. (Pearce later died of his wounds.)

Our jeep driver, Sergeant Ferris Webber, and his assistant Private Mestas took off down the road toward Anzio. A short distance down the road we ran into a barrage coming from our own artillery. Some jittery character must have called in our jeep as a German breakthrough! Webber called back to me, "Hold on! We're going through!"

From the Underpass to Anzio was about five miles. Less than halfway there we came to a British aid station on the left side of the road. Webber pulled in there, and we transferred all our patients. I told the station doctor to take particular care of Pearce, and he assured me he would. A high-top ambulance was there, and I wanted to use it to go back for my casualties at the Underpass, but the drivers were hiding and wouldn't come out. The doctor said he'd have them up on charges, but that didn't do me any good. I'd have taken the ambulance myself, but I'd never had a car and didn't know how to drive. That might seem strange in this day and age, but during the Great Depression, very few people owned cars.

Webber said he couldn't go back for the casualties because he had to get to a supply depot and hide the jeep and trailer before daylight. It was the only means he had of supplying the company, and he couldn't risk having it knocked out.

I rode with Webber for a mile or so down the road and transferred to an MP[1] jeep that came out of a side road. In another mile, I transferred to an ambulance heading for a medical clearing station. The ambulance driver wouldn't go back to the Underpass for my casualties and laughed when I said I'd get an ambulance at the clearing station.

I don't know how late it was, maybe near midnight when I went into the field hospital tent and raised hell with an officious orderly who refused to get the officer of the day. The commotion awoke the officer of the day, who got up from a stretcher on the floor. When I explained the situation at the Underpass, he

---

1. MPs are military police.

was very considerate. He got me two plasma boxes full of the supplies I needed and ordered the two drivers who had brought me to take me back for my men. That made me feel good, but I didn't laugh at them. I dozed inside the ambulance on the way back.

About fifty yards from the Underpass, we were stopped by an engineer lieutenant who told us he had just mined the roads three ways from the Underpass. We could walk through and carry back my wounded without setting off the mines, but the ambulance was too heavy.

In the field to our right was a farmhouse with a tank firing from behind it. The ambulance pulled into the field to get behind the farmhouse, but on the far side of the farmhouse it bogged down in mud. I asked the tank men to pull us out, but they kept firing away and wouldn't help. I don't know what they were firing at, but they hit our own tank, where I had left our wounded, and it burst into flames. For tank men, they seemed awfully damned frightened.

The ambulance drivers walked to the road and headed back to Anzio. The tank men had dug a spacious hole alongside their tank. I dropped into it and fell asleep to the lullaby of a barrage.

I awoke to a world of silence. The tank was gone, and the sun came out. That was rare, since we'd had almost continuous rain. The ambulance was still bogged down in the mud. I cut across the field and to the opposite side of the road, where there was a good ditch that I took toward the Underpass. A German spotter must have seen me, since shells started exploding around me, but none really came close.

One tank from the night before was gone, and one was still burning. I didn't see any of our casualties we had left on the road. I never knew what happened to them. Maybe the engineers from the night before took them.

About fifteen feet up the embankment left of the Underpass, two GIS waved to me from a cave. They had a big radio for I Company but were afraid to take it out there. I had my combat jacket filled with the two plasma boxes of medical supplies, and the radio was too heavy for me to carry. I got back to Cody, and he sent two riflemen for it. We really needed that radio because we had no communications with the rear. The tank behind the farmhouse was gone, as was the one that was bogged down in the field. The British ambulance in the ditch was still burning.

Cody set up the radio in a shallow cave dug out of a dry mound a few yards behind and to the right of his own dugout, which was under a tall haystack, and Stamas became the radio operator. When I went to the shed to unload my medical supplies and get my gear, the frightened boy from L Company was lying on top of it, dead. The only way he could have been hit was by our own artillery barrage the night before.

Things were a bit quiet for a change. I wandered into the open space between Cody's haystack and our company CP—a large standing foxhole holding Captain J. G. Evans, Lieutenant Sturtevant, and Captain Ralph Barker (my former platoon lieutenant), who was now commanding officer of L Company.

An L Company platoon was in the field in front of the farmhouse. A BAR lay in the mud. There were a couple of new GIS nearby, and I asked, "Whose BAR is that?" One said, "Mine." "What's it doing in the mud?" "It won't work. It's dirty." "Well, clean the damn thing!" "I don't know how." "Well, it's a good time to learn!" I handed him the gun, but he looked very worried. His buddy said, "I think I can help him," and they went off to a slit trench.

A young British soldier was standing nearby, and we got into a conversation about our chances. I don't know how it came up, but I told him that if I got killed, my mother would get ten thousand dollars insurance, more money than I'd ever make in my life. Coming from Depression jobs paying $12.50 a week, I wasn't far off. Who expected things to be better after the war? The Britisher got very nervous: "That's what my friends in the farmhouse said."

He was referring to eight British soldiers who were in the front room of the farmhouse when an eighty-eight went through the wall and killed all eight. I figured I'd leave the shaky boy alone and invited myself into Willard Cody's dugout under the haystack. He had plenty of room in his four by four by four-foot-deep excavation and didn't seem to mind the company. Since I was "detached" to I Company, Cody sometimes confided in me when he couldn't talk to other men of the company.

From Cody's dugout, I could work in all directions to answer calls of "Medic!" I had a lot of ground to cover to take care of my own platoon, Pearce's, L Company, some British, our weapons platoon, headquarters, and anyone else in the area. I'm proud to say that I never turned down a call of "Medic!" that I could hear. I expected to be killed at any second, but I didn't dwell on it, and the prospect never bothered me. I just didn't want to get killed hiding in a hole. I wanted to get killed doing some good for somebody.

I told Cody so many of my good friends were already dead that if there was a place where good soldiers go, I wouldn't mind joining them. I was thinking of the composer Richard Wagner's Valkyries carrying dead soldiers to Valhalla. Life back home during the Depression wasn't all that wonderful, and I didn't give a damn.

Early the next morning, Lieutenant Yentis stuck his head up for a look-see and a German sniper took him between the eyes. The sniper took three other men in the area but was shooting a mite high. One boy was creased across the top of his head and was unconscious. Two others were also creased but were conscious and in good condition. Behind the haystack was a long mound of earth that ran the length of the field. I suggested to Cody that we dig several slit trenches in the mound to hold wounded men until we could evacuate them. Cody assigned riflemen to do it immediately.

The sky turned murky gray again as the sun disappeared. The "safety" slit trenches worked well except for one casualty whose hole got blown in on him by an eighty-eight. He was one of our great tech sergeants, Kenneth Kindig, and he looked like a muddy apparition when he stuck his head into Cody's dugout and asked if he could come in. Of course we moved over and made room for him.

Late that night I heard Captain Evans yelling, "Put out that fire!" I stuck my head out and there, from the Bren gunners' hole, was a light that lit up the sky like a Hollywood arc lamp.

I ran over and looked in on three Britishers—brewing a cup of tea! "Your fire is lighting up the whole sky!" I told them. One said, "Do you think it matters? They do know we're here, don't they?" I said, "Why pinpoint it for them?" So they obligingly put out the fire.

The next morning the Germans hit us with a barrage that lasted over three hours.[2] They followed that with a massed infantry assault. Maybe they thought no one could live through their barrage or that anyone who did would surrender. But our men rose from their slit trenches and laid down such a rain of rifle and machine gun fire that the attack was stopped cold.

The Germans did the same thing for the next three days—the barrage and massed infantry attack. Each day we stopped them cold. Cowboy Wisecarver told me he'd had a duel with a German machine gunner for three days. On the fourth morning he got up really early but held his fire. Pretty soon the German wondered why Cowboy wasn't shooting and stuck his head up for a look. Cowboy told me he'd killed thirty Germans during their assaults. He said things so matter-of-factly that people didn't believe him. I saw him. I believed him. I knew a lot of great soldiers, but none greater than Cowboy. He eventually was awarded a Silver Star when, in my opinion, he should have received a Congressional Medal of Honor.

The German barrages and attacks wore us down to under half strength. A rifleman came to Cody's dugout to report that the Germans were sending miniature radio-controlled tanks filled with explosives across open ground. But he passed it off lightly with, "We're able to explode them with rifle bullets." After that one day, the Germans no longer used those explosive devices.

During that second day, a sergeant came back to Captain Evans when I happened to be nearby. He complained that German litter bearers wearing large red crosses on serapelike garments were

2. If you've ever seen a film of a World War I German artillery barrage blasting a battlefield with thousands of explosions (some of these actually filmed on the spot during the war by Hollywood cameramen), then you can appreciate what a three-hour German barrage looked like. Only a direct hit in a slit trench stopped our men. They fought back viciously as soon as the barrage ended.

slipping into German slit trenches, exchanging garments with men in the holes, and going on to the next hole to do the same thing under the guise of carrying off wounded when they were actually relieving men in broad daylight. Evans observed them for a few minutes, then ordered a machine gun to fire on them. That ended those shenanigans. Early that evening, Cody suggested we sandbag the entrance to his dugout. I got some wood from the shed and we piled three layers of sandbags on top, leaving just enough room to crawl in and out.

As we stood looking at our work, a British Bren gunner came over with a big white dog. It licked the hands of those who petted it and pranced lovingly like a puppy. I reminded Cody of the big white dog that had frolicked around our artillery in the rest area at Venafro before a barrage blasted the area. I told him that this was a German spotter dog and that we should kill it. Cody didn't have the heart to do it, and neither did the Bren gunner, so I borrowed his revolver, put it to the dog's head, and touched the hair trigger. The dog folded into the ground, and I threw it into one of the slit trenches we'd dug for the wounded.

The German observer evidently saw me kill his buddy and got mad. Early the next morning, as I was awakening, he called in an "Anzio Express."[3] I heard the thing coming all the way in. Its white heat set the top of our haystack on fire as it went through and exploded about five yards behind us. Wow! I'd been rocked by a lot of shells, but nothing like this! The concussion was like the end of the world. Cody and I coughed our way out of the dust-filled dugout. Every sandbag was shredded. The hay was wet and soon burned itself out. Stamas was just to the right of the explosion, and he and the big radio survived it. A barrage followed the Anzio Express.

During the barrage, Tech Sergeant Jim Rutledge from the L Company platoon came to our dugout for a tourniquet for one of his men. I grabbed my pouches and raced with him to his man, some twenty yards in front of our company CP. The fellow lay on

3. The Anzio Express was an 850-pound shell fired from a gun a bit larger than our 240-mm artillery piece.

the edge of a deep crater that must have been made by another giant Anzio Express shell. He had a puzzled look on his face. The concussion had yanked both of his legs out of his body; his thighs were shredded. I told Rutledge the boy didn't need a tourniquet. I slipped my hands under his armpits and dragged him down into the crater. He was dead before we reached the bottom.

Rutledge went his way, and I ran back to the haystack.

The next day, at the height of another German barrage, one of the British Bren gunners from in front of the farmhouse crawled to our dugout. "Your Sergeant Voth is hit bad. Will you come?"

I was out of the dugout in a flash and raced through the barrage to Voth's hole. I don't know how I never got hit. Voth, in a very deep slit trench, lay on top of a dead lieutenant, the one Sergeant Martinez had intimidated, but whose name I still didn't know.

With a nearly direct hit, Voth's wounds were as serious as Guy Pearce's. Pearce had a broken left leg; Voth's was severed at the calf and hanging by a sliver of flesh. He had a dozen other perforating and penetrating wounds. He was fully conscious and asked if I could save the leg.

I was going to finish the amputation but didn't for Voth's sake. I wouldn't have been able to anyway. When I pulled out the K-Bar hunting knife I'd used since Sicily to cut away clothes, I stared in disbelief. The blade was barely an inch long. A shell fragment the size of a .22 bullet was embedded in the leather scabbard and had broken the steel blade. I hadn't even felt it.

It was a morning of frustration. First my knife was broken. Then my medical scissors broke when I started to cut away Voth's clothes. Then one of the British threw me a bayonet that wouldn't cut butter. I had a terrible time trying to get at Voth's wounds. I did use his rifle to splint his leg. I yelled for Cody to bring me a litter from some we had behind the haystack. He brought it through that goddamn barrage. When he plopped down at my side, he said, "Why do you want a litter? We can't take him out of here."

I knew that a litter crew would be dead in four steps. "I need to get him elevated to shock position." We got Voth onto the litter, and Cody began digging a mound of earth on the "wind side" of him. I tore at Voth's clothing: a raincoat over an overcoat over a combat jacket, over two OD sweaters, over two OD shirts, over two long john tops. I tore all this away with my bare hands! When I finally exposed Voth's chest and stomach to work on his wounds, he screamed. I thought I had hurt him, but glancing up from his stomach, I saw an inch-square fragment from an airburst lying on his bare chest. I picked it up, and we both yelled when I dropped it. The thing was white hot! I brushed it off.

Staff Sergeant Emerson Voth died that evening before we could evacuate him.

Shortly after I left Voth, Captain Evans called for me. He wanted me to *crawl* to him. I crawled from the haystack to his CP and asked, "What the hell is this crawling business?" I hated to crawl. I always ran low to the ground. Evans said, "We're under too much observation." As the British Bren gunner said to me, they did know we were there, didn't they? But I didn't say that to Evans. I just looked disgusted.

Evans sent me about fifteen yards to his right, where a machine gunner was wounded. The guy had had an airburst to his back and chest. He was more scared than hurt, because the fragments hadn't penetrated, but he was in a panic because I hadn't arrived sooner. I calmed him down and ran back to the haystack.

The following morning, after their usual unending barrage, the Germans came at us en masse. I Company was now at less than half strength, and the Germans used leapfrog tactics that threatened to overrun us. We just didn't have enough men to hold them. That's when Stamas's radio saved us. He called in a barrage from our 158th Field Artillery Battalion and from British eight-pounders. Our barrage caught them in the open, as they were about to close with us, and slaughtered them. I heard Stamas yelling for Evans and relayed his message through the inferno, "Artillery wants to know the objective!"

Evans yelled back, "I can't see! There's too much smoke! Keep it up! It's wonderful!" Artillery kept it up.

The next day the skies cleared, and four P-38s came winging over, playing leapfrog sideways. They dived on the Germans close to our foremost riflemen and, with machine guns wide open, strafed the hell out of them and dropped wing bombs as they circled, and they kept it up until all their bombs were gone. They were deadly accurate. I had no reports of our own men being hit. The airmen were an all-Negro unit that had been over us since Sicily. Almost immediately after the P-38s were gone, the navy laid in heavy artillery along the Germans' flanks. They took one hell of a pounding. I have to admit that though I hated the bastards, I felt sorry for them.

The Germans' casualties that day must have taken the heart out of them. They stopped attacking. Stamas relayed a message from rear echelon: "You hold 'em one more day, and we'll have 'em licked!" That "you" and "we" really got me.

The next day (the seventh day, in my calculations), it was quiet. No German barrage, no assaults. The 3rd Battalion aid station sent me a new medic to replace Pearce (a week too late). I sent him back with a message that we'd be pulling out that night and they should be prepared to take care of our casualties.

At nightfall, a British unit started into the field to take over our holes. Some strode down the main road. One of our riflemen, who apparently didn't get the word that the British were coming, fired at them before he could be stopped. I had to treat one blown-off British ankle.

A private came back to Cody nearly hysterical. He didn't mind carrying out the wounded, but he and his buddies didn't want to touch the dead. Cody understood and said, "Okay, just cover them up."

There wasn't much left of I Company. Men had stayed in shallow, water-filled slit trenches and had severe cases of trench foot. Many of the wounded, using their first-aid packets, had just stayed in their holes and continued to fight. (Regimental history says there were sixty-eight of us still alive after the battle.) Everyone who could walk helped support someone who couldn't. Captain Evans and I carried Private Alcosure between us. Alcosure was the one who had gone with Lieutenant Blumberg to knock off a German machine gun and came to me to report that Blumberg was dead.

When we got to the back of the Underpass, British troops

that were to relieve us were in mass disorder. They were lighting cigarettes and smoking without hiding their light. They seemed heedless of the offbeat whir-whir of a German bomber overhead. We yelled at them to put out their lights. They did until we had gone past, then they lit up again.

When we arrived at our battalion aid station, we got word that the British were being blasted all over the crossroads to the Underpass opening. I should have gone back to help them, but I was disgusted at their stupidity and had other problems. The aid station was dark, and the personnel were all asleep. The doctor had paid no attention to my message to be ready to evacuate our wounded. Captain or no captain, I raised hell with him for not being ready for us. He acted as if I were a mental case and said to a station medic, "He doesn't understand the situation."

My God! We *were* the situation!

I Company, assisted by a platoon from L Company, a handful of British, a heavy machine gun from M Company, a couple of tanks, our 158th Field Artillery, and British eight-pounders, stopped the German drive to wipe us off the Anzio beachhead. From sergeants' evening reports, Cody told me we had killed over a thousand Germans with small-arms fire.[4] Add to that what our artillery, air corps, and flanking barrages from ships at sea had killed, and the Germans had had enough. Though they had us outnumbered, for the next four months they seemed content to just keep us locked-in on our beachhead.

At the Underpass, much of I Company consisted of new replacements in their first real battle. Our old-timers inspired them by example. I watched in awe as our tech and staff sergeants raced through barrages and German attacks to throw extra bandoliers of ammunition to their men. They were magnificent! I was proud of them all!

I'm not certain, but I do believe the army was ready to evacuate

4. Every evening of the battle, tech sergeants filtered back to First Sergeant Cody to inform him of what was happening in their platoon area and what was needed—food, water, ammunition. They also reported their casualties—dead and wounded—and how many of the enemy they had killed. These reports were recorded in the "daily report" that all first sergeants sent to regimental headquarters. That's where the "thousand enemy killed" information is from.

Anzio during our week at the Underpass. The way they locked us in by mining the roads and not sending replacements indicated that they had given us up for lost. Personally, I said "To hell with them! We'll win this war by ourselves!"

A few days after our return from the Underpass, my service with I Company ended. Our aid station doctor informed me that I was to join a new 2nd Battalion aid station that was being formed. I told him I wouldn't leave my company, and he threatened me with court-martial for disobeying. I appealed to Captain Evans, but he acted as if it was punishment for my insubordination. We'd been through so much together that I couldn't understand his attitude. When I appealed to Cody to keep me with the company, he wouldn't help. I later realized that Cody thought the transfer would keep me alive. He was a great one for trying to keep old-timers alive.

I was being transferred to 2nd Battalion because there was no 2nd Battalion! Everyone had been wiped out or captured at the Battle of the Caves while we were at the Underpass. They hadn't understood the seriousness of their situation when we went out to help them, and they said we weren't needed. During the following few days, they were overrun by massive German forces and paid dearly during some of the heaviest fighting of the Anzio campaign. Almost the entire 2nd Battalion was killed or captured. The whole aid station was captured because Captain Peter Graffagnino, MD, refused to abandon the wounded, and he had moved in that close to the battle. The lucky survivors from the Battle of the Caves were the wounded who had been evacuated.

I Company had moved to a rear area of Anzio. It had to take on about 150 replacements to bring it back to combat strength. The replacements we were getting were straight from the States and had no real basic training. What really scared me was that one boy I talked with didn't know who Hitler was. How can a man fight when he doesn't know who he's fighting or why? Many didn't know how to strip and clean their Garand M1 rifles; I sat with some to show them how. In an open field where our non-coms were teaching them infantry maneuvers, they were getting killed and wounded by German eighty-eights before they even got into battle. This was stupid, because we had divisions back in Naples, fully trained, who might have sent some of their men as replacements. They were back there during the four months we were at Anzio and weren't sent up until we were ready to break out.

When Leon Shapley, who was to be first sergeant of the new 2nd Battalion aid station, drove a jeep out to I Company to take me back to where the station was being put together, I was very depressed. I was honored and respected by the men from I Company. I always did my job to the best of my ability, no matter what the situation—artillery barrages, machine gun and rifle fire, mortars—nothing stopped me from getting to a wounded man. I had such a deep respect for the riflemen that they were my only consideration. Having come from the Great Depression, I placed no value on my life and didn't care whether I lived or died. The riflemen were in awe of how I did my job—and without a rifle for protection. Hell, I depended on them to protect me. Never again in the following year did I have this feeling of being honored and respected.

Shapley knew my feelings about leaving my company, and he was understanding. He was thirty-seven, ten years my senior, and a nicer man you couldn't find. On the way back, I became resigned to my position and said to Shapley, "We'll make this the best damned aid station there is." "Atta boy," Shapley said.

I saw all the weaknesses of our 3rd Battalion aid station. With the exception of a few like Shapley and Frank Riccata, most of the staff were cowards. Litter bearers refused to go onto battlefields to carry wounded. There should be hot coffee and a whiskey ration plus understanding and compassion for the wounded, sick, and fatigued. But it was many months before we got a doctor who saved our monthly two-fifths of whiskey strictly for the wounded. Earlier doctors let officers come in and drink it up when it arrived.

The new aid station was being created about five miles back of the front. Since the beachhead was five miles deep by fifteen miles long, we were practically on the waterfront. But I didn't see any water. I guess I was pretty psycho at the time.[5] I talked to no one, and no one talked to me. It was many weeks before someone told me they were afraid to talk to me, "'cause you were so mean." I didn't feel mean.

After a couple of weeks at the rear, about the time the new aid station was ready to go back to the front, a colonel from regiment came out to see me and said, "If you want, you can go back to I Company now."

I was confused about this sudden offer. Cody and Evans didn't seem to want me. I had been threatened with court-martial when I refused to leave the company. Now I was offered a choice. The peace and quiet of the rear was relaxing. I told the colonel, "I kinda like this soft life back here. Think I'll stay." That's all there was to it.

From then on, I no longer reviewed action from day to day, as I had done when I was with I Company. I've forgotten a lot. I do think there were times when I was out of my mind and didn't realize where I was. I do know that though I belonged in the station, there were times at Anzio and later in France and Germany when I was out on a battlefield caring for wounded. No one ever stopped me; I came and went as I pleased.

When the aid station was formed and moved to the canals near the front, we had a fine doctor named Catey. He was a kindly man, possibly in his late forties (which is too old for combat). One day we got a casualty in deep shock. The blood had drained from his veins to the pit of his stomach, and Catey couldn't find a vein to insert a plasma needle. The boy died, and Catey sat with his head in his hands and cried.

We put some of my ideas about a "good aid station" into practice. Newly arrived litter bearers, two of each, were sent out to the companies as permanently detached before they learned to be afraid. Things were okay for a short while, but then the companies sent them back. Though the riflemen wanted their medics, a

---

5. I use "psycho" (psychoneurotic) loosely. Losing friends in combat can make a person so vicious that only his close companions are safe around him. In France I became more relaxed, but there were still times when I could turn mean. (I'm normally a very mild person.)

couple of guys with a litter seemed like tragedy waiting to happen. But we had good men, and they weren't afraid to go out to bring in the wounded.

We couldn't carry out some of my ideas at Anzio because we were practically on top of riflemen—it was that crowded and there was so little room. Having hot coffee available wasn't always feasible when shell fragments were ripping through our tent. The ideas worked better in France and Germany, when the aid station wasn't so close to the front.

I'll try to keep some kind of chronological order to events of my second year. What follow are ramblings about what I remember.

One morning, shortly after moving up to the canals with Catey, I saw a squad of riflemen pitching pup tents on an open slope about fifty yards from our aid station tent. This was suicidal with Germans able to observe every foot of our beachhead. A large puff of smoke rose from the spot. I shouted to a new litter bearer, "They're hit! Bring a litter!" and I raced off clutching my medical pouches.

Only one shell had exploded, and fortunately no one was killed, but four were wounded. As I worked on one in his pup tent, one of his buddies shouted a warning. A bandolier of ammunition lying on the ground was on fire, and bullets started exploding. "Throw dirt on it!" I told the frightened kid. He did and put out the fire. These were very green riflemen indeed. All the wounded could walk, and the litter bearer and I led them back to our aid station. They were mighty lucky. At Anzio, with German high-ground observation, it took only one man in the open to bring in a barrage.

Another day I heard a loud explosion about fifty yards down the canal. I went for a look-see. A German shell had made a direct hit on one of our 105-mm gun emplacements. The artillery piece was upended, and four dead artillery men lay scattered about. Somehow people think that being in the artillery is safe. Hogwash! When a big gun goes off, it does a lot of damage and shortly becomes a target for a counterbarrage. The 158th Field Artillery unit attached to our 157th Infantry Regiment saved us on several occasions, but it took enormous casualties.

Engineers are due much praise. No army in history attempting to capture Rome from the south had survived in the Pontine Marshes at Anzio: mosquitoes and malaria wiped them out. We survived for four months because Mussolini had dug canals to drain the marshes and turn Anzio into a fashionable tourist resort. But he hadn't completed the job, and the water-filled canals were still a malaria hazard. It seemed strange, almost foolhardy, for engineers to be wading waist deep spraying chemicals to kill mosquito larvae while shells were bursting around them and riflemen were engaged in combat nearby.

When Captain Catey was relieved, we got a doctor who flew in directly from the United States. He didn't have combat clothes, not even a helmet, and arrived in a brand-new dress uniform, shiny and clean as though just off the shelf. He brought an oversize leather duffle bag. Things were quiet that day, and this gentleman hadn't the faintest notion of where he was. Why officers in the rear hadn't taken him in hand, I don't know. Clearly he was a mistake. We fed him because he had no rations, and he was oblivious to what was going on. When one of our own shells screamed overhead he panicked, jumped up, and ran around like a chicken with its head chopped off. He was so terrified when more of our shells went overhead that he was totally out of control. He was gone by evening, and we were without a doctor for a couple of days. Then we got Captain Chalstrom.

Chalstrom was a lean, physically fit young doctor from the South. He had a nice mustache. He also liked mint juleps! In early spring the ground at Anzio was covered with soft green grass, and sprigs of mint grew there. Chalstrom gathered mint, added 190-proof medicinal alcohol and a few ration hard candies for color, and voila! Mint juleps!

Chalstrom also enjoyed going barefoot in the grass and liked a game of horseshoes. The horseshoes and posts came from empty artillery cases that had each held three shells. A long steel rod ran down the center of the cloverleaf-shaped casing, and there was a small horseshoe-shaped washer at the top and bottom of the case. Hence horseshoes! Unfortunately, on two different days shell fragments whistled over the grass and cut across the top of

Chalstrom's feet. The wounds were no worse than simple knife cuts, and Chalstrom dressed and ignored them, but I quit playing with him. It was a silly way to get wounded or killed.

One morning I awoke in my slit trench. The sun was shining, and I said to myself, "What do you know—it's my birthday and I'm still alive! It was March 14, 1944, and I turned twenty-seven.

Just about that time First Sergeant Leon Shapley got hit. He was standing on the edge of our canal when an eighty-eight exploded. I was in a slit trench only a few yards from him when it came in. I got to Shapley in seconds, and Chalstrom and Robert Smith came from the aid station tent. Chalstrom did all the work while we tried to comfort Shapley, who had a gaping stomach wound. Thank heavens for Chalstrom.

Shapley recovered from his initial shock and was calm when he spoke directly to me. "I heard it coming all the way in but was too lazy to duck." His tone was rueful. "And just when I was going to get my stripes back." Shapley had had some kind of altercation with that damned 3rd Battalion aid station doctor, and the doctor had demoted him to private. But he was the best man they had to lead the newly formed 2nd Battalion station, so he was a private acting as first sergeant. His stripes were pending, and getting them back meant a great deal to him. We couldn't evacuate Shapley until nightfall; ambulances in daytime were fair game for German eighty-eights. However, he was getting the best possible care from Chalstrom, who confided to me that he had serious doubts about Shapley's survival: "The fragment severed his spleen."

I didn't know the spleen from the liver, but Chalstrom's tone worried me. We were later informed that Shapley had died in a field hospital. He was a rare, good man.

When we were in a canal at Anzio, about the time Shapley was hit, I had been having battle dreams. Strangely, I never had dreams during the year I was with I Company, but now, in the comparatively safe spot at Anzio, I started dreaming.

I had received a letter from my brother, who was serving in the Pacific as an artillery observer with the infantry. In his letters, he told me he had gone through the jungle and climbed a tree overlooking a Japanese encampment, called in artillery, and listened to them screaming below as they blew the place apart. In my dreams my unit was fighting Japanese, and they were always trapping us and shooting the hell out of us. After about a week of this, I awoke one morning with a big smile. In my dream that night, we had trapped the Japanese and blasted the shit out of them. I had no more battle dreams after that.

Late one morning, the phone in the aid station tent rang. Colonel Brown, at regimental headquarters, had a headache and wanted some aspirin. I was alone with Chalstrom, so guess who got elected to go? I hadn't the faintest notion of where headquarters was, but it had to be behind us. I took off on a nice, sunny morning and hadn't gone more than a couple hundred feet when an eighty-eight came screaming in. I got jackhammered into the ground but wasn't wounded, so I went on my woozy way. I felt like the character in Elbert Hubbard's short story "A Message for Garcia" who didn't know who or where Garcia was but still delivered the message.

I don't know how, but I did find the regimental HQ and gave Colonel Brown his aspirin. The sour-faced so-and-so didn't even say thanks. It's the least he could have done for almost getting me killed.

That wasn't the end of it. I was told to wait for dark before leaving the area. I got lost in the pitch-black night and didn't know where the hell I was. I kept stumbling and found myself facing a machine gun with two GIs on it. I was lucky I didn't get shot, since I was coming in from the German lines. I asked the gunners if they knew where the aid station was, but they hadn't the faintest idea. So I bunked down with them in their oversized nest.

I awoke early the next morning, said good-bye, and walked over their mound and directly into the aid station tent—only twenty feet away. (I amazed myself with my homing instinct.) As I opened the tent flap, Chalstrom shoved a man's leg in my face and said, "Bury this someplace." A fine greeting after wandering around the German lines all night. Chalstrom must have had a lousy night too; he had just finished the amputation when I arrived.

One day, about the third month on the canals, I was ordered to go to regimental headquarters, where I found out I was to receive a Silver Star for action a year before at Castel de Tusa, Sicily. Medals had been awarded in Sicily while I was in a North African hospital with severe trench foot.

A formal ceremony is supposed to accompany the awarding of all medals. This "formal ceremony" involved a one-star general with his aides, all probably from a ship three miles out at sea, who came scurrying through the underbrush and trees hiding the headquarters. They looked nervous as hell—as though they had just come from an exhausting battle with the German army— read citations to six of us gathered there, pinned medals on our chests, and let us in on a secret. "Men," the general said, "you'll be out of here before the mosquitoes get too bad." Then he and his aides scurried away as if the Germans were on their tails.

Headquarters wanted us to wait until dark to return to our outfits. They were afraid too much movement would expose them to German observation. I talked to a doctor, a major. I told him it wasn't right that most combat medics with the infantry troops were only privates. They were respected by riflemen and frequently took on the duties of noncoms. They risked their lives daily with the infantry, but it was men in rear aid stations who were getting ratings and the extra pay that went with it.

Said the thoughtful major, "We give the men in the aid stations the rank and additional money *because you medics in the field have the opportunity to win all the medals.*" Can the brass really be that stupid?

It happened again! On the way back to my aid station, I got lost in the pitch dark. While I was stumbling around, a GI combat patrol came down a draw. The sergeant in charge said to me, "What the hell are you doing out here?" (Actually, he whispered.) I figured they wouldn't know where the aid station was, so I whispered back, "I'm looking for I Company." The sergeant pointed off to his right and whispered, "It's back there. We're inside the German lines." "Good-bye, fellows," I said and took off in the direction he had pointed. I eventually found the station and showed off my medal. When the battalion chaplain, Raley, came around, I gave him my Silver Star to send home.

One day we moved our aid station to a building that had formerly been occupied by the 3rd Infantry Division. We called the building the castle. It had two stories and a tower that British soldiers used for observation. (In his autobiography, *To Hell and Back*, Audie Murphy describes his experience in the Castle.[6] It also appears in the movie based on his book.) Fifty yards in front of the building was a German tank bogged down in mud.

The second floor had the best space for casualties, and we occupied it, though we had no casualties while we were in the building. One quiet afternoon, however, the British occupying the tower came scrambling down to us. It was rare to see frightened British, but these guys were scared! An eighty-eight had gone right through their observation tower without exploding. We all moved down to the first floor. In the kitchen, a small basement had been dug into the floor by the men of the 3rd Division, or by prisoners. They had blasted through concrete into the dirt and had a shelter about five feet deep. I mention this only because the building was interesting, as were the British. Nothing dramatic happened to us here.

Axis Sally, a German radio propagandist, the equivalent of England's traitorous Lord Haw-Haw and Japan's Tokyo Rose, was broadcasting daily reports of Anzio activities that were accurate beyond comprehension. She had information about every unit on the beach, knew the names of company commanders and newly arrived officers, reported the disposition of troops, and even listed our casualties. No one could figure out how she got all this information.

The nerve center of all operations at Anzio was in a building in the city, where the brass had its fingers on all beachhead activities and where all front line troops sent their daily reports. In this vital

6. Audie Murphy was a 3rd Division sergeant (later lieutenant) who was the most decorated soldier in European conflict. He played himself in Hollywood's film version of his autobiography.

headquarters, *how could they have not checked the basement?*
Yep! There were German spies down there listening to every word
uttered above them and radioing every word to Berlin! I don't
know what genius figured that out and cleaned them out.

One day I was riding in the jeep in the rear area when we
passed an airfield used by Spitfires. German bombers had hit them
the night before. It was sickening to see the wreckage of those
beautiful planes all over the field. I loved Spitfires.

I don't remember when Captain Chalstrom left us or the name
of the doctor who immediately followed him. I do remember that
it was about this time that I made my contribution to medicine.
We had a casualty in deep shock, and the doctor couldn't get
plasma into his collapsed veins. The doctor was frantic. I said,
"Why don't you cut for it?" The doctor looked at me, amazed,
and said, "Why didn't I think of that!"

He sliced into the arm with a scalpel, used a forceps to pick
up what looked like a large corrugated chicken vein, inserted the
needle, taped it down, and let the plasma flow. He did the same
with the other arm, and color flooded back into the face that
had gone dark gray, near death. We saved the boy. After that I
told every new doctor about this procedure, and each one reacted
with the same surprise and immediately did it. We saved many
lives this way. I've lived long enough to learn that this medical
procedure was officially sanctioned in the 1960s. We were doing
it in 1944! So much for my contribution to medicine.

I'm going to skip ahead to the drive out of Anzio in May 1944.
It was the most furious action since the battles at the Caves and
the Underpass. The beach was jammed with new troops from the
Naples area, plus all kinds of additional support. The scale of the
attack was so huge it would take a Homer to fully describe it,
but Flint Whitlock does a very good job of it in his book about
the 45th Division, *The Rock of Anzio.*

Early during the drive out of Anzio, I stopped to care for a
wounded man and fell behind my outfit. I caught a passing ambulance from the 85th Division (new to the beach) that was moving
up. The driver and his assistant both bitched to me, "When do

we get relieved? We've been here ten days!" They're bitching to me, a guy who's been at Anzio for four months?

The Germans had set out thousands of antipersonnel mines. Step on one, and you lose a foot. The mines were particularly heavy in an old cemetery area. Captain Ralph Barker, my former platoon lieutenant, lost a foot. An I Company acquaintance who visited Barker in a field hospital expressed sorrow at his tragic wound. He told me Barker passed it off with, "Oh, hell, that's the foot that was always getting cold."

Dorsey Tash, a former medic with I Company who had been pulled back into the aid station before the Anzio landing, went out into the cemetery to help a wounded man—and also lost a foot. I had never thought much of him, but he finally came through.

The action was fierce! I found myself out on a battlefield again. This time I gave aid to an old-timer who had been with me in the 28th Division before we became part of a thousand-man complement sent to bring the 45th Division up to combat strength before it went overseas. His name was Wilkerson, and he had gone from private to tech sergeant. Cody once told me he thought Wilkerson was the best soldier in I Company. That's saying a lot, considering all the great soldiers we had. I first met Wilkerson when the 45th Division was on final maneuvers before shipping out. A field judge had tagged him as having a "cheek wound," which I bandaged. Now Wilkerson had been shot lengthwise through the ass. I laughed when I reminded him, "In the States I bandaged one of your cheeks, and now I'm bandaging another."

I'm trying to limit this memoir to specifics—what I did or what I saw personally, but a "worm's-eye view" is limited to what was in front, in back, or to either side of me. So I feel compelled to include some accounts from my close friends. Having seen most of them in action at one time or another, I know they downplayed rather than exaggerated the experiences they related to me.

During the drive out, I Company's Tech Sergeant Youtsey was with Wilkerson when a German killed him. Wilkerson saw the German run from one hole to another. He told me he grabbed Youtsey's tommy gun and put it on full automatic as he ran to the hole he saw the German disappear into. As he stood over

the hole, six Germans had their hands up trying to surrender. "I emptied the whole thirty-shot magazine into them!"

It was shortly after this that I found Wilkerson lying alongside a railroad track and bandaged his "other" cheek. I'll come back to him later.

The action was nightmarish. Our aid station was practically on top of charging riflemen. We moved up with them as they moved up. Never again, in the following year, did we get this close. For a short while we occupied the area where the 2nd Battalion had fought the Battle of the Caves four months earlier. Our aid station was in one of the larger caves. Fighting the previous day had been so furious that for the first time, to my knowledge, we couldn't find all of our wounded. Chaplain Raley spent the night roaming the battlefield looking for casualties. He didn't find any, but in the morning he came in with four prized Lugers that he took from the bodies of dead German officers.[7]

Late that morning I cared for a staff sergeant with only half a face. His whole jaw had been blown away, just like the boy on the first day into the Venafro Mountains and the British soldier at Anzio. The sergeant was heroically calm and showed no fear. There was no bleeding, and all I could do was sprinkle on sulfa powder and tie on a Carlisle bandage. Such wounds are heart wrenching.

One day I found myself in a huge cavern where the regiment had set up headquarters. The entrance was partially blocked by a German Tiger tank that had tumbled from a ledge above and rested on its turret.[8] Whether there were dead Germans in the tank, I don't know. Maybe they were still alive. There was no way to open the turret to find out.

It was an unhappy day for me. The regiment's Colonel Church was on a radio with I Company Captain J. G. Evans. The headquarters had some kind of speaker system, so I could hear both

7. The Germans did not call this pistol a Luger. They referred to it as a "Pistolen-08." It fired 9-mm bullets.

8. The German Tiger tank was *big*. It had four-inch-thick steel fenders protecting its treads. It fired an 88-mm shell that could knock over almost anything we had. It took our 105-mm artillery shell to knock it out.

ends of the conversation. Colonel Church was ordering Evans, "Take that hill!" Evans was pleading, "Colonel, if I take that hill I'll be cut off and captured! I have no flank protection!" Church's response, "I don't give a damn! Take that hill!" Evans took the hill, but he and the remnant of survivors were captured, as he had warned.

Evans and I may have had disagreements, but I respected him as a great soldier and a great leader. The Germans evacuated him so fast that he wound up in a prisoner-of-war camp in northern France. The following year the regiment liberated him, and he went to a hospital and home.

On the day of Evans's capture, I developed a strong dislike for Colonel Church. I thought him arrogant and self-seeking. Naturally, the army promoted him to general.

On June 2 the regiment, assisted by units from the newly arrived 36th Division, captured the high ground at Velletri. We could look down on most of the beachhead. I guess it was from here that Bill Mauldin was inspired to draw one of his famous cartoons, with Joe and Willie looking down and exclaiming, "My Gawd! There we wuz and here they wuz!"

We took over an old two-room railway station. The main room was used for treatment. I walked into the second room, bare but with very black walls, and the walls began to move. They were covered from floor to ceiling with *fleas*! I got a can of DDT spray, showered it throughout the room, and ducked out the door. A few minutes later I went back in. The room was clean, but a thick line of dead fleas bordered the base of the walls. This was my first experience with DDT spray. We always used DDT powder in the seams of our long johns and other clothing, but that was to kill lice.

From the Velletri station, I went out a couple of times to assist casualties. One day it was one of our old-timers, the tall, lean, good-looking Johnny Cohen. When the outfit had landed in North Africa and had toughening-up maneuvers after three weeks on shipboard crossing the Atlantic, sand in shoes caused serious blisters. I remembered putting my tried-and-true blister bandage on Johnny's feet. Now he had a chest wound from an airburst. I wanted to get litter bearers, but Johnny insisted on walking, so I put my arm around him and walked him to the station.

Across a dirt road from the aid station, a Red Cross truck was passing out coffee and doughnuts to a long line of German prisoners. We weren't set up yet, so I went across the road to get some coffee for Johnny. An American girl serving the line refused me. "This is only for German prisoners," she said. The Germans were down below killing our men and had wounded Johnny, and this pretty girl passing out coffee and doughnuts to Germans gave me a dirty look as if I were a moocher. To this day I have never donated one cent to the Red Cross, though I've been a frequent blood donor.

On another day, I went out to take care of a German para-trooper that an old friend from I Company had shot out of a tree. The wound was minor. My friend let me take the German's paratrooper helmet and "Gott mit Uns" buckle and belt. After the fall of Rome, I was able to send them home to my fiancée's father. The German spoke some English. He said he had never seen anything like our assault out of Anzio—and he had been on the Russian front. His Mauser rifle had a broken trigger housing held together by a piece of wire. "If we had your weapons," he said, "we would win this war." German prisoners all tried to flatter us, but as soon as they saw we weren't going to kill them, they became arrogant SOBs.

While we were at Velletri, tragedy struck. I Company was in a gully when German tanks appeared above them and fired on them point-blank. Our aid station was filled with casualties. I was torn between working on the wounded and going out to help the company. I stayed with the wounded.

The division was doing well. We had the Germans backpedal-ing fast, though there were small pockets of strong resistance, but it was never a picnic—we suffered heavy casualties.

One evening our station was on top of a small hill. As it grew dark, brilliant flares went up all around. It looked as if we were surrounded. A new infantry lieutenant who happened to be present figured he'd cheer up our concerned faces. "Men," he said, "we've got them right where we want them—all around us!" It wasn't funny at the time, but the next day we learned that the flares were from surrounded pockets of Germans signaling for help.

We captured Rome on June 4, 1944. "We" included all the divisions that had come onto Anzio for the drive out and all the support units attached to those divisions. I believe the 45th Division and the 3rd bore the brunt of the action. We did the impossible! We captured Rome from the south, a feat not equaled by any army in history.

Yet on June 6, 1944, the dramatic invasion at Normandy relegated the Italian campaign to forgotten history.

Rome was an "open city." That meant the Germans didn't defend it and we didn't blow it apart. We didn't parade into Rome; we chased the Germans north around it. They were backtracking so fast we couldn't catch them, and we bivouacked in a field not too far north of Rome.

From this bivouac area we were allowed to visit Rome. A truck from the regiment took a load of us. I spent most of the day hobbling around the city—Hadrian's tomb, an ancient temple, the Colosseum, and the Catacombs—everything was open to us. I marveled at Saint Peter's Basilica, which is so big that it houses seven altars where hundreds of people can attend services at the same time. In the center is the pope's pulpit, framed by golden columns that reach to the heavens. The ceilings of inlaid tiles are of such magnificent colors and blends that they are more like paintings than mosaics. Everything is of such huge proportions that it is difficult to realize how large the place is.

At noon Scottish Highlanders, their kilts swaying, marched around the great plaza playing bagpipes. Never before had I enjoyed bagpipe music, but I've loved it ever since in the same way I learned to enjoy cowboy music from fellows wailing their songs across the hillsides when our kitchen trucks brought up their guitars.

I really couldn't enjoy the art and antiquities as I might have in peacetime. After the many months of combat, being in the mountains most of the time, wet, miserable, freezing, tired, sleepless, stinking from dried blood, seeing my buddies killed or wounded—all this seemed unimportant. It was like looking at Mount Vesuvius and seeing "just another goddamn mountain."

A beautiful cobblestone promenade borders the Tiber River that runs through Rome.[9] It was peaceful strolling along the tree-lined boulevard on this beautiful day, heading back to the truck that would return me to my bivouac area. But three drunk GIs ahead of me were disturbing my cherished peace and quiet. The middle one was a real bastard. Anyone approaching from the opposite direction he shoved off into the gutter. These guys must have been new to combat or were typical of rear echelon characters who moved in after the action and acted like conquering heroes.

An Italian teenager and his pretty girlfriend were strolling along, enjoying each other as lovers would, when this punk, only a few yards ahead of me, viciously shoved them off the sidewalk. I figured the Italian boy was big enough to take care of himself, but when a doddering old man leaning on a cane got the same treatment, I became livid. Now I was only a step or two behind the bastard and said, "You son of a bitch!"

The bully turned to me and started to say, "Who called me . . ." I jabbed his mouth so hard I knocked out his front teeth. He was a bloody mess, and I was ready to knock the shit out of him when an MP jeep came along. The bully's two friends took him under each arm and led him away in the opposite direction.

By the time I got back to our truck, I was in trouble. The blow had split my left hand between my little finger and the next one. The cut was swollen and painful. Cody was there and put iodine on it, but by the time I got to our aid station my hand was twice the normal size. We had a new doctor, Captain Irving Teitelbaum, who evacuated me immediately and said, "Be sure to tell them it's a human bite."

I spent two weeks in a field hospital in Rome. My evacuation tag with "human bite" seemed to interest several nurses who

9. We crossed the Tiber when we chased the Germans north and west of Rome. From my reading of history, I expected it to be a real obstacle. Where we crossed it was so dried up that I stepped across without getting my shoes wet.

came to look me over. They must have thought I'd been bitten by a girl, but why should that interest them? I never told the real reason for the injury, fearing a fight would be logged in my record as "bad time," so I made up a cock-and-bull story.

When I finally returned to my outfit, it was bivouacked in a field near Naples. There I was greeted with the news that I'd been promoted to sergeant. I also learned that we were in training for the invasion of southern France.

6

The Invasion of Southern France

The division made its fifth combat landing on August 15, 1944, a little east of Toulon in southern France. Again we were lucky. The Germans weren't ready for or expecting us, and the navy laid down such a tremendous barrage that we had no real opposition.

While waiting to disembark, I saw for the first time salvos of rockets launched from barges. It was also the first time I experienced German "flying bombs," which didn't seem at all accurate. At least they didn't hit us!

Off the beach, I was standing nearby when a lieutenant shot a German sniper out of a tree a few hundred feet away. The bullet took off the man's whole lower jaw—the fourth such casualty I treated.

From St.-Maxime, near our landing site on the Mediterranean coast, we serpentined westward across the south of France, going through or bypassing a dozen towns until we came to Pertuis, which was almost due north of Marseille. Here we had our first real rest stop. When our aid station jeep pulled into the town square, it seemed as if the whole population came out to greet us. What excitement! We were the first Americans they had seen, and they were hospitable beyond belief. They set the tone for our experience in France. To me it was like coming home. I loved France. I loved the people. Over a year in Sicily and Italy had left me cold and unfeeling. I cannot explain the change that came over me.

Our aid station set up in a combination barn and garage off the main square. We were invited into friendly homes. I was billeted in the second story of a simple home off the square opposite our aid station. A young couple with an infant gave me a bed. They were ecstatic over my gifts of K rations,[1] especially a box of fresh coffee, which we had plenty of in the station. They hadn't tasted coffee during the five years of the German occupation. When they boiled some, they used the grounds over and over until there was no color in the water. They didn't know what to do with the canned milk I brought for the baby. I showed them how to mix it with water.

My two years of high school French slowly came back to me, but I must have sounded like a real foreigner, because I could remember only the present tense of verbs. My vocabulary was very limited, but I got so I could get the gist of what people said to me if they spoke slowly. The Mexican, Spanish, and Italian Americans who got by so easily and fluently in Italy were lost in France because the pronunciation was totally different. I was frequently called on as an interpreter when Captain Irving Teitelbaum wasn't around. He spoke fluent French, Italian, and German in their Swiss dialects.

First Sergeant Harold Smith, now a lieutenant, was billeted in a home near mine. When he was invited to dinner, he asked me to come along to interpret, and I was invited to eat. Monsieur Joseph was a well-to-do farmer before the Germans took over. He and his wife had a daughter about twenty, a son about sixteen, and a younger daughter about three or four. They seemed to have plenty of food. The first course, which I thought was the main meal, was cabbage cooked with small pieces of pork that tasted like no cabbage I had ever tasted. It was heavenly. That

1. Daily K rations came in three boxes, approximately six by eleven by two inches, marked breakfast, lunch, and dinner. Once when I gave one to a Frenchman, he exclaimed, "Quelle organisation!" The rations contained a tuna-sized can of some mysterious, inedible substance (except for the cheese with bacon), a small container of four cigarettes, a matchbook, toilet paper, a can opener, hard candy, a hard chocolate bar, an envelope of lemonade mix or powdered chocolate, an aluminum packet of Nescafé (instant coffee), and hard tack (biscuits). The rations were double wrapped, with one light cardboard box inside another. The inner box was completely wax-covered. By feeding small pieces of it to a fire, one box could bring a canteen cup of water to a full boil—its most valuable use. The other main use of this box was as a urinal when you couldn't expose yourself from a slit trench. Fill it and toss it out.

was followed by thinly sliced beef with vegetables and French bread and red wine. The dessert was cooked cactus apples with eau-de-vie, a fruit brandy, that was fire all the way down.

Having lived seven years in an orphanage of sorts, a family sitting together at a dinner table was my idea of heaven. The older daughter, Michelle, seemed so beautiful that I was dumbstruck. She transformed me from a Mr. Hyde to a Dr. Jekyll. My hatred for Germans had made me so mean it poisoned my system. I hadn't realized what sort of person this hatred had turned me into. When I returned to the aid station, Captain Teitelbaum and others were so amazed at my transformation that they couldn't believe I was the same man. Neither could I.

The next day, Harold Smith drove his host out to visit his orchards, which he hadn't been able to see for some months. Michelle went along, and I went too, as interpreter. The orchard was a few miles out of town, and after we got out of the jeep and looked around, the father wanted to see another of his holdings. Smith drove him, but Michelle and I stayed behind. She said, "Promenade avec moi." As we walked around the orchard, she took my hand; it felt marvelous that a girl would hold my hand. Our touching didn't go beyond that—she was so clean, and I felt so dirty. My clothes must have smelled to high heaven; I hadn't washed them since leaving Italy. Michelle seemed to take no notice. Though she was inviting, I did not make love to her. I was engaged to a beautiful girl who was writing me letters every day. I couldn't be unfaithful to her, though months of combat were making it difficult to remember what she looked like.

Pertuis has a fourteenth-century cathedral. Michelle introduced me to the presiding priest. Compared with our two-hundred-year-old missions in California, which we consider old, this was an eye-opener about antiquity. Michelle gave me a picture of herself with her brother and her little sister and a small pocket book in French titled *The Joys and Sorrows of Love*. I still have both, but my French has never been good enough to read the book.

Pertuis was typical of the many small French towns we liberated. Excited natives, local and from outlying districts, rejoiced that the Germans were gone. Many Frenchmen were eager to join us to fight the Germans. As we progressed into France and casualties mounted, we gave them weapons and supplies. They showed great courage in combat. Even children as young as twelve or thirteen wanted to join us, but their first encounter with German artillery terrorized them. We sent them home.

If we stayed long enough in a village or town, we were treated to the experience of a town crier. There were no newspapers, and all news came via the crier, who arrived in the village square on a bicycle. He beat a snare drum to draw the attention of the townspeople, who eagerly awaited his news. I don't know what his sources were, but he read items from a sheaf of papers, tapping his drum once at the end of each item, then got back on his bicycle and pedaled to the next village.

Shortly after leaving Pertuis, my regiment was attached to Brigadier General F. B. Butler's task force. We were supposed to throw a net across the Rhône valley to destroy German forces in the south and keep them from retreating north. Damn! It seemed as if ten German divisions hit us and went right through. We did inflict some damage, but our casualties were fearsome. Our aid station worked endless hours caring for them. Shortly thereafter, the regiment was returned to the division, and we began a long running battle chasing the Germans up the Rhône valley. They retreated in an orderly fashion, setting up plenty of rear-guard action to slow us down. By late August 1944, we had liberated many small towns and villages.

At one small farm village, Captain Teitelbaum came into the station after visiting a local doctor. The captain told us, "The doctor said the Nazis rounded up all the local Jews and forced him, under threat of death, to drain all the blood out of their bodies for whole blood for wounded Germans." This was probably the best-kept secret in Hitler's army. Our government should have spread the word. Think of all the pure Aryan supermen who would have committed suicide when they found they had Jewish blood. It might have ended the war months earlier.

On another day we set up shop in a small restaurant at the crossroads of a town square. In the basement Captain Teitelbaum found a bottle of wine that he proclaimed was a marvelous vintage year. So he set an elaborate table with a tablecloth and invited Harold Smith and Robert Smith to join him. He didn't invite me.

A short time later, a Frenchman came into the station looking for a syringe. He had a bottle of medicine that he wanted to inject into his baby for whooping cough. The only needles we had were what I called "horse needles" for injecting plasma. Since I spoke a little French, Teitelbaum sent me to do the "shooting." Jack Miller, our jeep driver, drove me and the Frenchman to his home. He must have been wealthy, because "home" was a chateau of astonishing beauty. The interior looked like a Hollywood movie set—winding stairway and all.

The baby, an infant of less than a year, was in an upstairs bedroom. When I started to fill the needle with the medicine (which Teitelbaum said wouldn't do a bit of good but would make the father feel better), the Frenchman looked horror-stricken. "Lavez les mains!" he ordered. (I was about to inject the baby without washing my hands. We rarely had soap and water, and I always sterilized my fingers by brushing them with iodine swabs.) The adjoining bathroom had soap and running water, and I obligingly washed my hands. When I tried to inject the baby, his skin was so tough that I had a terrible time penetrating his little bottom. Finally, it was done. The Frenchman gave us a glass of wine, and we drove back to the station.

There we found a tragic mess. The Germans had left an 88-mm gun in the town, facing the German lines. A new lieutenant thought it would be great fun to shoot it at the Germans. He didn't bother to check the bore, which the Germans had plugged. There was a shell in the breech. When he pulled the lanyard, the gun exploded, killing him and everyone with him and wounding a dozen other men, who were brought into the aid station. The wounded were on litters all over the floor. Teitelbaum had plasma going into two of them. I held one bottle, and Clifford Bingham held the other. Then the real hell broke loose as German shells began exploding in the square. When the first one hit the upper part of our building, everyone disappeared except Bingham and me. We stood holding the plasma bottles. A second shell hit the building, and a third exploded in the cobblestone courtyard out back. When the next one again hit the upper building, I told Bingham, "Discontinue the plasma! Put tables and chairs over the wounded in case the ceiling comes down!"

After we had done this, I went out back to the cobblestone courtyard. All the tires on two ambulances, our jeep, and our jeep's trailer were flat. Captain Teitelbaum was under the nearest ambulance with a jagged steel spike in his chest, but he was still alive. I went along the courtyard to find men to help. In a space between buildings I found about six litter bearers and ambulance drivers. They were so scared that none of them moved when I told them I needed help to get Teitelbaum into the station.

Finally the two Smiths showed up, and with Bingham they brought Teitelbaum into the station. They weren't doctors, and there wasn't anything they could do for him. I cranked the phone to headquarters and told someone, "We've been hit pretty hard down here. We need a couple of ambulances and a doctor!" An officer, I don't know who, got on the phone and said, "Where's Captain Teitelbaum?" I glanced at the table, as the Smiths threw up their hands in despair. "He just died," I answered. Silence at the other end of the line.

I went out back and told Jack Miller to put new tires on the quarter-ton so we could move up the hill to the textile factory where headquarters was. He refused. He was too scared. "Okay," I said. "Drive up with the flats and change them up there." The barrage was over, but he and the others were still scared. When you're with a rifle company for a year, barrages are practically everyday occurrences. There's nothing to be afraid of if you have a ditch to jump into. That's what everyone in rear echelon needed— a year with a rifle company. I was surprised that Robert Smith had panicked and hidden. He'd been with a rifle company for a year and had been awarded the Silver Star for valor.

For a while, the only doctor available was our dentist, Mitchell Sack. He was a great dentist, but he didn't know anything about trauma medicine. I remembered him from Sicily when, after the campaign, he set up in our olive grove. While his assistant foot-pumped his drill, he did such fine work as root canals when pulling a tooth would have been easier. I asked him why he took such pains with the men, and he replied, "When I get home, I have a practice to keep up. I have to keep my hand in."

We went about our business as usual. Normally we had two doctors in the aid station, but a few weeks previously, one had evacuated himself with severe asthma. I don't remember his name because I don't remember names of men I didn't like. He was a good doctor, but after Rome, he'd threatened to court-martial me because I disagreed with him about a Greek philosopher. He must have been nuts.

I went to regimental headquarters to get away from the SOB, meaning to rejoin I Company as a rifleman. Cody was there, as was Harold Smith. Cody said to Smith, "If you send Joe out to the company, I'll kill you!" I was surprised, because I had never heard Cody so threatening. He was still trying to keep me alive.

Getting back to that long-absent doctor, I was alone in the station when he strolled in a couple of weeks after Teitelbaum died. "Where's Irv?" he asked. I didn't try to spare the doctor's feelings. "He got killed a couple weeks ago when the Germans shelled our station."

The doctor's face went ashen. He turned around and left the station, and I never saw him again.

7

Rambervillers, France, to Aschaffenburg, Germany

The Germans never stopped us until we got to Rambervillers. It was late September 1944 when the 157th Regiment liberated the city. German opposition on the outskirts stopped us but also gave us a breathing spell.

We set up our aid station in an abandoned two-story hotel in the northern part of the city. Next door on the street was a family of four. The mother, a seamstress, was assisted by her daughter Yvette and daughter-in-law Marie. The girls were both in their mid-twenties. The Germans had occupied France for about four years before we got there. Marie's husband, unable to find work, had volunteered for labor in Germany. Marie asked me to look for him when we got to Germany. Talk about needles in haystacks.

Yvette told me that the hotel we occupied was owned by Jews who had been taken away by the Nazis. I told her, "Je suis aussi un Juif." It didn't matter to her. She loved all Americans; we were their liberators. French families who lived in two-story homes on the cobblestone street visited us with smiles and open arms.

I regret that I can't remember the name of our French family. The mother and two girls sat sewing in a living-dining room with a large window that faced the street. There was a piano against the wall opposite the window. When we were invited to dinner our aid station doctor, a wonderful man named Arthur Murray, played a great jazz piano.

Just before we entered Rambervillers, I found a puppy in a field, cuddled up with a dead German soldier. I gave her to Robert Smith (Smitty), who was about to go out of his mind after a year and a half of combat. The puppy was like a shot of adrenaline to him. He named her Lena after a prostitute he had met in Naples. Lena was the life of our aid station. In winter, Harold Smith made her a warm jacket from a piece of blanket. When she got worms, we gave her 190-proof medicinal alcohol. It cured the worms, but she was very drunk, weaving her way across the floor to her bunk (a litter). She looked very funny with a small Carlisle bandage tied to her little bottom when she came into heat. She was accidentally run over by an army truck and was in such bad shape that Smitty had to shoot her. Smitty was inconsolable until I found a family with a litter of pups very much like Lena and gave him one. That did the trick. He called her Lena II, and we had her for the rest of the war. The army wouldn't let us bring her home, so we had to leave her in France.

The Germans were not backtracking as fast as previously; they were now putting up aggressive resistance. Their artillery zeroed in on the city and shelled it frequently. Our street was not hit, but the city's main square, about a mile away, was blasted on a Sunday morning when it was filled with people who had just left church. The French carried on their own emergency services, evacuation, and hospitalization without calling on us. I marveled at how organized and independent they were within a week after we had liberated the city.

There was a small quadrangle in our street across which the father had a shop. I went with him one morning and watched him solder and repair worn pots and pans. His was a general repair shop, and he was a very good artisan. He was husky, with a curled mustache, and had been an artilleryman in World War I. He told me about the daily thousand-round barrages that had turned forests and fields into empty wastelands. He knew what war was.

Late one afternoon, a terrified neighbor from down the street, an organ maker, came running into our aid station calling for me. "Sergeant Joe! A soldier with a gun at my house! Come quick!"

Harold Smith, Robert Smith, Gordon MacPhail, and I raced home with the Frenchman, clambered up the stairs, and froze near the top. There, in a small hallway, was a drunk GI with his arms around the man's wife, pointing a cocked .45 at the head of a baby in her arms. He was demanding wine. They had no wine. The drunk seemed to recognize us as friends and said, "These goddamn Germans got wine!" He didn't know where in the hell he was.

The woman was terrified, the baby was crying, and the Frenchman was horror-stricken. I was afraid the gun was going to go off. I spoke softly to appease him. "Hey, we got lots of wine down the street. Come on." Both the Smiths and MacPhail soft-talked him into drinking with us, and talk of wine sank in with him. He released the woman and let us lead him away.

When we got him to the aid station, we gave him a cup of wine laced with a couple of tablets of "blue heaven" (sodium amytal) that put him into a deep sleep. When he woke up the next morning and we told him what he had done, he was filled with remorse. He went back to the organ maker's family, apologized more by his looks than by speech, and returned to his unit at the edge of the city. I once wrote about this incident in a short story I sent to an agent, but he said it was "too contrived." Not a lot about war is believable.

Our French family was amused by French communists who periodically dashed through the streets in automobiles converted to steam power, since gasoline was unavailable. The autos had wood-burning boilers fastened to the back. Every once in a while one would stop for someone to jump out and add wood to the firebox, then take off again. The autos carried as many as a dozen whooping, hollering, rifle-waving men that the city folk looked on as phony "partisans" who made a great show while doing nothing more than dashing back and forth from the combat zone to the safety of the city.

Earlier, in France, after leaving Pertuis and getting about halfway to Rambervillers, we encountered the true French fighting men, the Maquis. They were organized units loyal to General Charles de Gaulle. We supplied many of them with abandoned equipment from our casualties, but they fought independent of us. When the regiment headed for Grenoble, a historic Middle Ages city where the Germans were committing horrible atrocities against the civilians, we took up a position on a mountain overlooking the city and prepared to attack it in the morning. Unknown to us, the Maquis attacked that night and captured Grenoble. They saved us a lot of casualties.

The evening before our scheduled attack, Gordon MacPhail and I were scouting out a place for our aid station on a hill overlooking Grenoble. A large house on the hill turned out to be an orphanage for the children of civilians massacred in the city. I still have a picture of MacPhail surrounded by smiling children.

We stayed in Rambervillers most of October 1944, while the regiment had a rough time breaking through the German defenses. In November we were attacking through the Vosges Mountains and forests. It was a cold, rainy winter, and German artillery tree bursts were a worry. The Germans exploded shells into the trees, and the fragments showered down on the GIs. If they couldn't put heavy covers over their slit trenches, there was no protection from tree bursts. We found many men with their skulls split open.

After Rambervillers, towns went by as in a nightmare. The fighting became fierce for the riflemen. We medics were never up close as we had been at Anzio. Usually we were comfortable several hundred yards back in some farmhouse or café. My trench foot was always painful, but I rarely had to walk; I could ride in a jeep.

In mid-France in winter, three of us were trying to get across a quagmire of calf-deep mud to reach a farmhouse that might be used for an aid station. I don't remember how we got into that field afoot, but I do remember that the muck was almost impossible to get through and that a German observer picked us out and started throwing eight-eights at us. The explosions were getting damn close as we neared the dry clearing around the farmhouse. The three of us slammed into the door with a crash that sent us sprawling into the barn-size room. At the far end, leaning over a large washtub and scrubbing clothes on a washboard, was a woman of about fifty. She merely glanced at us as though this were an everyday occurrence, calmly said, "Bonjour," and didn't miss a beat of her scrubbing.

In northern France we had an aid station set up in a café. I'd been out for some reason and walked in to find four aid station men sitting on the floor near the door playing poker. Across the room, on a litter, was a wounded Negro soldier with no one attending him. I asked, "Who's taking care of this man?"

"Dad" R——, the obvious leader of this group, spoke up: "Hell, he's a nigger! Shot himself in the foot." (We called him "Dad" because he was about thirty. Months previously he had begged me to bring him into the station and away from his company medic job. I obliged.)

I was so angry that I said, "Dad, maybe you can beat me up, but let's step outside and I'll give you a chance to do it!" He just sat there and didn't take me up on it. I went to the soldier and took care of him myself. I didn't blame him for shooting himself in the foot. Why should he risk his life fighting if he was going to be treated as a second-class citizen?

Near the first of November 1944, we went into a rest area near Martigny-les-Bains in eastern France. On November 14, the 3rd Battalion of the 157th Infantry Regiment had a parade formation before Lieutenant General Alexander M. Patch, commanding general of the Seventh Army. This formal ceremony awarded I Company the Presidential Unit Citation for its Battle of the Underpass at Anzio in February 1944.

The rain had stopped, but the field was muddy. A wooden platform had been built so that Patch and his entourage wouldn't get their feet muddy. Before passing out the Presidential Citations, Patch awarded some individual medals. Willard Cody got a Legion of Merit, a most beautiful award for outstanding leadership, one of only sixteen earned in the entire regiment. Those of us who had been in the aid station when Captain Teitelbaum was killed received Silver Stars, and the marvelous combat soldier, Major Felix Sparks, was the surprised recipient of the silver oak leaf that promoted him to lieutenant colonel. General Patch personally presented all these awards. An army photographer took individual pictures. Mine appeared at Christmastime 1944 on the front page of the *Los Angeles Daily News* with the caption "Christmas Decoration." Patch was on his platform; I was standing in the mud.

Then came I Company's turn. The entire company was in formation. The men who had been at the Underpass were in the front row. General Patch had a cardboard box full of citation ribbons that he pinned on each man as Cody introduced him by name. I was the last man in line, and when Cody introduced me as the company medic, General Patch looked astounded. There were only thirty-seven left of the sixty-eight who had returned from the battle. "Is this all that's left?"

Patch was insulting when he pinned the citation on me. He said, "Medics in the Pacific carry weapons!" Maybe I was wrong in detecting a sneer. I should have responded as I once did to a medic who had laid aside his pouches and picked up a rifle to participate in a "turkey shoot." When his buddies came into the aid station with him and praised him for his using a rifle, I very quietly said to him, "While you were shooting a rifle, who was taking care of your wounded?" Battles and wars are won when every man does his assigned job to the best of his ability—whether it's killing the enemy or pounding a typewriter back in the States.

General Patch started to make a speech to the assemblage. He began, "I'm often asked when this war will end. It will end when all soldiers stand up like this company." The company's standard bearer, who apparently hadn't heard the command "at ease" and was standing at attention throughout, fainted and fell flat on his face in the mud. Patch's next words were, "I suppose the kindest thing I can do right now is to dismiss this formation." And he did.

Damn it! We needed to be told how good we were!

One day on the way to Alsace, we got a wounded boy with a compound fracture of his right leg. The splintered bone was protruding through his thigh. Captain Murray fitted on a traction splint—a long basketlike device that extended from the crotch to the foot. He tied a traction strap to the boy's ankle. We looked like a toboggan team. I sat on the floor and held the boy by his armpits, and MacPhail sat behind me and held on to my waist. At the boy's foot Captain Murray sat tying on the traction strap while Harold Smith held on to his waist. Robert Smith stood by. It took tremendous strength to pull on the traction strap so as to bring the bones into line and tie off the strap to the end of the splint. We pulled with all our might, and Captain Murray was about to tie off the strap when it broke. The boy screamed as the bone ripped back into his thigh. Robert Smith immediately handed another strap to Captain Murray, who wasted no time in retying it. He pulled out the leg again. This time the strap held, and the boy breathed a heavy sigh of relief as the pain diminished.

Civilians don't know who is winning the battle around them. When we drove the Germans out of one small Alsace town, the populace cheered from their balconies, hauled in their Nazi flags, and put out their flags of Lorraine. When we pulled out on a flanking maneuver within a few hours, the civilians thought the Germans were coming back. In went the Lorraine flags, and out came the swastikas. I didn't take offense; I thought it was both humorous and sad.

In another small farming village in Alsace, our infantry had captured about twenty Germans and penned them in what looked like a horse corral. German tanks came up on the hill overlooking the village and laid in flat trajectory fire. Some shells exploded in the corral, killing and wounding many of their own men. Our farmhouse aid station was filled with wounded Americans and Germans. One German lad I worked on cursed me and all Americans. I got the gist of what he was going to do to us when they won the war. I shut him up with a few morphine syrettes.

When most of our casualties, American and German, had been cared for, I was called to a farmhouse next door. A young German soldier of about eighteen lay on a bed with what looked like a piece of steel an inch square embedded in his chest. I thought it was a minor penetration. Using forceps, I thought I could ease it out. I gently moved it back and forth, but it kept coming and coming and coming. I had gone too far to stop now. Some of the medics and litter bearers watching began to curse me. They wanted to take him to Captain Murray, but I knew the doctor still had his hands full. I paid them no mind. After all, I was a sergeant and they were privates—and this was a German enemy.

He didn't seem to be in pain. His color was good. He wasn't spitting blood, so the steel fragment hadn't punctured a lung or touched his heart. The more I worked the fragment, the more relieved the boy looked. When I had the thing out about five inches, I told one of the medics to stand by with a Carlisle bandage in case the wound spurted.

I pulled it out another couple of inches, and the wound did not bleed. What I held in my hand looked like a sharp-pointed railroad spike, only narrower. I tied it to his evacuation tag so the doctors in the hospital could see what was in him. I could only wish it had been this way with Johnny Matthews and Captain Teitelbaum. The German looked fine. My audience did not applaud. They hated me.

Someone in I Company called me to look at a very strange German casualty. They were in a wooded area. The German lay at the base of a tree with several GIs around him. His pants were unbuttoned, and in full view were his penis and testicles. The German, a pudgy lad, looked terrified. I guess he thought he had lost his "treasures." Had he been able to see his wound he wouldn't have been so frightened. The skin that held his testicle had been sliced open as if by a razor, and his ball lay outside its sac. There was no blood, and the testicle was undamaged. I merely poured on sulfa powder, spread the skin, slipped his ball back into its pouch, and taped the thing shut.

Some casualties I cared for, mostly civilians, were so horrible that I cannot write or talk about them, even sixty years later. When I think about them I cry. But I'll try.

A French couple, probably in their late twenties, and their baby were brought into our farmhouse aid station. They had so many wounds it was a wonder they were still alive and conscious. They lay on litters on the floor, almost touching. The young husband had multiple lacerating, penetrating, and perforating wounds and broken limbs—as did his wife. Both of her breasts had been amputated as though surgically removed. There was no blood.

Dr. Arthur Murray was bent over them doing all the emergency work while others of us stood by. He thought the couple might survive but held out no hope for the mutilated baby. Three aid station workers came in to gawk at the woman. I ordered them out with a fury. While Dr. Murray worked, the woman and her husband looked at each other across their litters—it was a look of love that I've only seen in movies—and they reached out and held hands.

We were in the town of Bitche, not too far from the German border and directly west of Karlsruhe, Germany, when the Germans struck up north, in the "Bulge." No one seems to know that they hit us almost as hard here in what we called the "Bitche Salient." The difference was that in the Bulge the Germans went through green troops. Here we were mostly seasoned veterans who bounced a little and then hit back.

Here I experienced my first German rocket. I was lying in bed in a farmhouse when the rocket came in so fast it was ahead of its sound. It landed in a culvert back of the house wall and went off with such a terrible explosion that I bounced nearly to the ceiling, came down, and rolled under the bed. I've been through thousands of explosions, including the Anzio Express, but this one took the cake. Two GIs who were in the "safe" concrete culvert were killed. I didn't see Captain Murray and went outside to look for him, fearing he'd been hit. He came walking toward me very gingerly. The damn thing had rocked him, but he wasn't wounded.

At this farmhouse, I was stunned by a casualty who was an old friend from I Company. I had evacuated him in Italy. His name was Benzer, and he came back after the fall of Rome. He thanked me profusely for getting him a long hospital rest. Now, only a few months before the war would end, he had taken a tree burst in the Vosges and was brought in with his brains hanging out. I didn't recognize him until I checked his dog tags. Incredulous, I exclaimed to Captain Murray, "This is Benzer!"

Captain Murray was sympathetic. "Just put him aside and let him die," Murray said. "If he lives, he'll just be a vegetable." As many as I witnessed, I could never come to grips with the death of a friend.

Above this village was a medieval castle, and Captain Murray decided to move the aid station there for better protection from the shelling. The castle had a dirt-filled moat and a dirt road leading into the main gate. A narrow, winding tunnel led from the gate to the castle grounds. All along the tunnel were side rooms with narrow slits through which medieval archers could fire on invaders. The castle was large enough to hold the entire village, and most of the people came up every night to be safe.

One morning, Captain Murray and I were looking over the castle parapet when the Germans began shelling. They were firing low against the solid granite walls, and for the first few explosions below us we could see mere specks of dust fly off the granite. Then we moved to safer ground.

From Bitche we went on maneuvers to practice crossing the Rhine. We crossed in small assault boats near Karlsruhe, during the night on March 27, 1945, without a single casualty. An advance squad of scouts from the 157th went the length of the German defenses, which were dug into the lee side of earthworks running the length of our area. The Germans were caught sleeping. The scouts raced along the embankment, threw grenades into open machine-gun emplacements, and wiped out the entire opposition.

8

Aschaffenburg, Germany

We advanced on Aschaffenburg (in western Bavaria, a bit south of the dead center of Germany). On the way there we captured several small towns. In one farming village I was greeted by an Australian with a big smile who said, "Howdy, Yank! Where you been these past five years?"

The Australians were marvelous. They'd been captured on Crete five years earlier and had been used for farm labor ever since. As far as I could determine, they had the most freedom of any prisoners I saw during the war. They were too far from home to try to escape. They made themselves useful but right at home. The one who first greeted me relaxed in an easy chair before a fireplace in the farmhouse living room. Two small children bounced on his knees while he puffed on a pipe, and the farmer's lovely daughter sat nearby. The Aussie looked more like the lord of the manor than a prisoner. It didn't take a genius to see that the children were his, as was the farmer's daughter.

The Aussie told me that when they first arrived as prisoners, a German guard killed a close friend who had trouble keeping up. "The bastard shot him for no reason! Later we found out from the wrapping on a Red Cross relief package that we had certain rights under the Geneva Conventions. We were entitled to celebrate our national holidays. So one day we refused to work to celebrate "Billy Roark Day." That was the buddy the German had shot.

All the Australians stuck together in their demand, and the village mayor didn't know there was no such national holiday.

Frustrated, he gave them the day off. He couldn't afford to antagonize the prisoners; farm labor was essential, since all the young German men were off to war.

The Australians asked us not to molest any of the villagers, because they had been treated well. But they didn't like the mayor, so they threw him into the fountain in the town square. That's all the revenge they wanted.

My background before the army was in the legitimate theater. I nearly starved in New York in 1938–39 trying to break in when, at the height of the Depression, almost nothing was being produced on Broadway and thousands of actors, dancers, and entertainers of all categories were looking for work that wasn't there.

But to get back to the war—Gordon MacPhail and I were alone in a German farmhouse aid station. He was on night duty, since I had been on all day and it was my turn to sleep. When I woke up in the morning, MacPhail asked me if I'd had a dream. I didn't understand his question and asked why. "Well," he said, "in the middle of the night you got up and told a little joke, sang a little song, and danced a little dance, then went back to sleep." Gee! If a Broadway agent had been there, I might have gotten a job.

In early March 1945 we headed for Germany's Siegfried Line (Germany's response to France's Maginot Line). I don't remember my twenty-eighth birthday on March 14, but we went through the Siegfried Line March 17–20 and crossed the Rhine on March 27.

Aschaffenburg was the last city we captured before I was hospitalized. General George S. Patton, Third Army commander, had sent back word that he had captured the city, so we thought we'd have an easy time. Like hell! He had bypassed it and its garrison of four thousand dyed-in-the-wool Nazis.

Patton had captured a bridge across a river that flowed alongside the city. It was damaged, but it held up under our vehicles. When our riflemen started up an inclined road leading into the city, however, Nazi soldiers turned them back with intense fire.

The only good thing about that first day was that one of the companies captured a warehouse on the outskirts that contained about thirty thousand cases of the finest wines, champagnes, brandies, and you name it—all looted from countries Germany had overrun. All the company jeeps backed into the warehouse and loaded up.

A problem arose. Some GIs got drunk, forgot where their booze had come from, and wandered up the road into the city for another drink. Our aid station was set up on a slope where we could clearly see that road, and we saw a couple of men fall as snipers' bullets hit them. The Germans were using wooden bullets like those I'd seen at Comiso, Sicily. Though they weren't deadly, they splintered, and every splinter had to be removed to avoid infection.

Our airplanes dropped leaflets on the city that warned of bombing and shelling to come. Civilians were guaranteed passage out of the city, but civilians who started down the road to us were shot dead by Nazis. That stopped their exodus.

A weeklong barrage of Aschaffenburg began. Our main target was a castle that had four towers and held four thousand disciplined Nazis. Each day another tower disappeared. Riflemen entered the city under our barrages and began taking the place apart house by house. Nazi resistance took its toll.

Our aid station entered the city and set up in a two-story house owned by a family of doctors. We used their second-floor operating room. A photo on a mantle showed the father and son in German uniforms with swastika armbands. They were off at war somewhere. Fortunately the wife was also a doctor.

On our first day there, Captain Murray was out when we got a casualty in deep shock. None of us were qualified to cut for the vein to insert plasma, and I was afraid we were going to lose the boy when the woman came in. She spoke English, and I asked if she could help with our patient. She obliged and inserted the plasma needle on her first attempt, saving the boy's life. She continued to work with us as several other casualties came in.

When all were cared for, the woman asked me if she could go to her room, which was just across a small hallway. I was surprised that she asked permission. "Of course," I told her. She asked if she could close her bedroom door. I was puzzled. I suppose German propaganda left her expecting to be raped by "savage Americans." "Certainly," I said. "Close it and lock it, if you like. No one will bother you." No one did. Maybe it happened somewhere, but during my two years of combat I never heard of anyone in my outfit raping anyone. I think it was a hanging offense.

I was down on the street when the Germans from the castle surrendered, all who were left of the four thousand. A German officer, marching alongside his captured men, was ranting and raving at an American officer escorting the column. From his tone, he was probably telling the officer what he was going to do to him after they won the war. I wish I could recall who our officer was. It warmed my heart when he hauled off and kicked that German in the ass—so hard that the guy looked embarrassed and shut up.

It was my first experience of seeing American soldiers looting. Several smashed the windows of a jewelry shop and stole everything on display. I was in a room in a German headquarters building when several men from I Company broke open a safe that contained hundreds of thousands, if not millions, in German payroll currency. One gave me a handful of several hundred thousand marks. It was good money, but I didn't know it and gave most of it away for souvenirs. I still have some of it. Had I known it was good, I could have bought some hotels and cafés and other property in Aschaffenburg.

I too became a thief. I stole a woodblock print of Aschaffenburg that was on the aid station wall in the doctor's home. I still have it.

Berlin was several hundred miles northeast of us, and we headed for it with very little opposition. Things were getting rather hazy. We were on a hill looking down on a long prairie, and one night I saw something I had never seen before. Low clouds hung in the night sky, and the British bounced arc lights off them and lit up the ground below like daylight. The whole German army was scrambling like panicked ants, wildly dashing in all directions to find concealment. Then the artillery opened up.

When we were in the Bitche Salient I had an opportunity to become a lieutenant. Word came to us that *anyone* who had come overseas with the division could go back to the rear for ten days of training and come back to the outfit as an officer. We were losing officers so fast that Command was desperate. I told Harold Smith to sign me up, then I had second thoughts and changed my mind. What was I thinking? I could barely hobble because of my trench foot. My back pain was killing me. I was always getting lost and didn't know where I was. I'd only get men killed.

One evening in a small village in Germany, I was asked to be the medic for a platoon-sized patrol that was going into enemy territory. They had lost their medic, and I never turned down such requests.

The platoon was gathered around its lieutenant in a small courtyard for a final rundown of the operation. I was sitting on the cobblestones about ten yards from the group (none of whom I knew) and noticed that one man had a concussion grenade attached to his rifle. It stood out above his head. A concussion grenade is fired with a blank cartridge, sails toward its target, and explodes on contact. In the crowd, someone's rifle must have hit the grenade, because it exploded on the rifle. It killed the GI, the lieutenant, and half a dozen men around him. Sitting on the ground, I was below the explosion and wasn't injured. I don't recall how many men I gave aid to; by that phase of the war I was in a daze most of the time. There was no patrol that night.

It was in a small village east of Aschaffenburg that I finally wore out. I had such severe low-back pain that when I sat I couldn't straighten up until I'd hobbled halfway across the room. I couldn't stand, turn, or walk without such torture that I could hardly bear it. But quitting never crossed my mind. I was there to see the damn war through to the end.

When Captain Murray noticed my plight and told me he was going to evacuate me, I didn't put up a fight. I was totally useless with pain, and there was no longer any German opposition. I knew the war was nearly over.

I let myself be loaded into a truck with truly wounded men and felt like a deserter—the way I had felt in Naples when my trench foot was so painful that I let them load me on a plane to fly to North Africa.

We could have been in Berlin well before the Russians, but politics stepped in and the whole Seventh Army was turned south. While I was being flown to France, and during the first few weeks of my hospitalization, the regiment captured Nuremberg on April 21, 1945. It then liberated the infamous Dachau concentration camp on April 29 and wound up the war in Munich in May.

From the airplane, the countryside was beautiful in the spring. I was flown from somewhere around Bruckenau, Germany, to France, where I was loaded onto a hospital train headed south. I don't know what hospital I was in when we got news that Franklin Roosevelt had died. A somber mood prevailed. Some newer men thought it might make a difference in how the war would go. They didn't know the war was just about over.

Within a few weeks, when I was in Reims, France, Germany surrendered unconditionally. Among the old-timers there was no jubilation, no wild celebration. At last the damn war was really over. I had given it my all for two years. Now maybe I could go home—if they didn't send me to the Pacific to finish off Japan. I had no heart for that. I was sick of it all. Though a psychologist in the hospital assured me I had plenty of points to go home, I was leery that some character might put my name on the wrong list. I didn't realize how psycho I was.

My paralyzing back pain eased off little by little. In the hospital I was X-rayed, but only army technicians looked at the X-rays while I was there, and I doubt they knew how to read them. Later a psychologist told me the pain was due to too much combat and was all in my head. Hell! He didn't know my head from my lower back—that's where all the pain was.[1]

I spent about three weeks in that Reims hospital before being transferred to another hospital for relocation home. There I found

1. Over sixty years later, at the behest of my congressman, Howard Berman (D-CA), the Veterans Administration sent me to a doctor for evaluation. Among other war-connected injuries, she found a slipped disk that was pinching a spinal nerve. The VA finally admitted that my injuries were service connected and compensated me from the time Berman wrote his letter in 2001. Had the compensation started when I first filed for it in 1945, I'd be a rich man.

that Captain Murray was a patient—he too had finally worn out. He seemed in good spirits when I visited and was happy that I had come to see him. When my first daughter was born, he sent a silver spoon.

There I also came across Bob Shane, our mortar man, who had survived two years of combat. He had been with I Company when it liberated Dachau and recounted the gore he had witnessed— the rail cars loaded with skeletal bodies, the ovens, the dying inmates—the horror of it all. He said men from I Company went berserk, rounded up all the prison guards they could find, lined them up along a canal, and machine-gunned them.

Shane also told me he was present near Velletri, off Anzio, when German tanks bushwhacked I Company in a gully. He saw Charles Kroetsching's intestines fall out when a shell fragment ripped open his belly. This was the first I knew that Kroetsching was back with the company and had been killed. I was shocked! He was my closest friend, and I hadn't been there to help him.

At this relocation center, I also met with Tech Sergeant Wilkerson, whom I wrote about earlier. He said, "I'll always remember you on Bloody Ridge [Sicily]. You looked like a bloodhound with your nose to the ground, coursing back and forth across the mountain, smelling out wounded men." Wilkerson had been awarded the Distinguished Service Cross. After I dressed his buttock on Anzio, he was hospitalized in North Africa. There he went AWOL to a local town, and when he got back an infuriated Jewish doctor threatened him with court-martial. So Wilkerson hated Jews: "All the goddamn Jews are back in the rear or in the States while we're doing the fighting!"

I looked at him in disbelief. I led him to a nearby counter that served coffee. While we drank, I spoke softly. "Wilkerson, do you remember Private Shulman on Bloody Ridge? A German bullet shattered his hand and his rifle. He was going down to get another rifle and 'be right back!' He was Jewish.

"Remember Lieutenant Blumberg? He took a couple of men and went after a machine gun that hit him in the face. He was Jewish.

"Remember Sammy Shacter, who was running a message for

Cody when an eighty-eight took off half his hand and broke his leg? He was Jewish.

"Remember Lieutenant Yentis? At the Underpass on Anzio he stuck his head up for a look-see and a sniper hit him between his eyes. He was Jewish.

"Remember our great Doctor Teitelbaum? He was killed in southern France when the Germans shelled our aid station. He was Jewish. Most front-line aid station doctors were Jewish.

"Wilkerson, most of the Jews are not back in the rear. There are only five million Jews in the United States, including women, old men, and children. Jews are in combat out of all proportion to their numbers. If the Germans capture any of them, they don't go to prisoner of war camps. They go to concentration camps.

"And Wilkerson, I'm a Jew." I left him there, silent, and walked away. I never saw or heard from him again. He was one helluva great soldier. I hope I enlightened him about Jews in combat.

It's time to bring this memoir to a close. From that relocation hospital in France, I and many others were loaded into a boxcar, a World War I "forty and eight."[2] It was so crammed that we had to take turns sleeping on the crowded floor. We rode to the outskirts of Paris, where we stopped and were told not to leave the area because we'd be pulling out any minute. I was anxious to get home, and I believed it. I'm ashamed to say that now that I had given my all and the fighting was over, I and the others were treated like shit. Our boxcar sat on that siding for three days while they kept telling us we'd be pulling out "any minute." I would have loved to spend those three days seeing Paris.

Eventually we wound up in Belgium, and after another week we were loaded on the first liberty ship that had been refitted for troop transport. We left from Antwerp and passed the White Cliffs of Dover. That's as close as I came to seeing England.

It took three weeks for our ship to cross the Atlantic. As we approached the Statue of Liberty in New York harbor, all the

---

2. A "Forty and eight" was a World War I railroad boxcar in France that carried eight horses and forty men. They were still using them in World War II.

ships and boats around us blew their horns and whistles, and people filled the windows of buildings ashore and waved madly. I didn't know this was a reception for returning veterans—no one told us—and I stood on deck wondering what all the hullabaloo was about and who it was for.

We sailed down the coast, disembarked, and eventually took a military train to Fort MacArthur in San Pedro, California, where I had been inducted three years and three months before. It was July 28, 1945, when I got my walking papers. *It wasn't until then that I truly believed it was all over and I was home!*

But coming home wasn't like a Hollywood movie with troops marching down Broadway and thousands of flag-waving, shouting people. It was a very lonely, empty feeling.

I had phoned my fiancée from Fort MacArthur that I was home and she should meet me at the bus terminal in downtown Los Angeles. She sounded very excited, but I was not.

I had just come from a miserable war. I was psycho without realizing it. The transition from war to peace was so sudden that I was in a daze. Nothing was real.

I tried to hitchhike to Los Angeles, but no one would give me a ride. I'd been in combat for two years, and nobody would give me a ride. (Later I realized that drivers were probably tired of giving rides to thousands of GIs from Fort MacArthur.) I don't remember how I got to Los Angeles; it must have been by bus or red car.[3] I got to the terminal in the evening, and there outside was my beautiful fiancée, Betty. It was not a Hollywood reunion with two lovers charging into each other's arms. I stood for a moment just looking at her. I was bashful; I'd been having nightmares that she would no longer want me. I still wasn't sure this beautiful girl would have anything to do with an ugly character like me, with no prospects. It must have been strange for her too. She hadn't seen me for two years, and I don't know what she saw in me.

---

3. Until a few years after World War II, the "red car" was a rapid-transit electric streetcar in Los Angeles and outlying communities. I won't go into the politics of how the petroleum industry tried to rid Los Angeles of all electric streetcars to promote the sale of automobiles and gasoline.

She was so beautiful that she could have married anyone of her choice in Hollywood, but she had waited for *me*.

She came to me, and I gave her a light hug and kissed her cheek. Later, a lifelong friend of us both told me that despite endless offers, Betty never dated anyone and waited for me. She had a map of Europe on the wall of her office in the advertising department of Bullock's Department Store in downtown Los Angeles, and she moved pins in it to follow news of my division through Sicily, Italy, France, and Germany. All the girls in her department had adopted me as their soldier in combat (that was the patriotic thing to do during the war) because they all loved Betty. When the *Los Angeles Daily News* ran a picture of General Alexander Patch presenting me with my second Silver Star, the office girls saw it before Betty did and brought it to her. She immediately got the eight-by-ten original that the *Daily News* had used. They gave it to her freely because she placed a lot of Bullock's ads with them.

I stepped away from Betty and gave her a chance to back out of our engagement. (I told you I was psycho.) Then I said, "Let's get married next week, or I'm going back to New York." I had a sister there and a few friends from my starvation days. To my amazement, Betty agreed.

It was July 28, 1945. We were married on August 4.

9

Afterthoughts

The tragedy of war, for those who have fought and lived through it, is that it never ends.

During the sixty years since 1945, not a night has gone by that I haven't lain awake and fought the war over and over. I think of my close friends who died, and sometimes in the middle of the night I cry for them. I never cried during the war.

When I came home from the war and an old friend advised me against getting married because times were so rough, I told him, "If I can win the goddamn war, I can win the peace!"

I don't believe I won the peace until the last few years of my life. I've always had to borrow money or work two jobs to pay the mortgage, feed, clothe, and shelter three children and a wife, and pay taxes and utilities. How or why my wife put up with me for fifty-six and a half years is one of the mysteries of womanhood.

It took three years after the war for me to adjust to civilian life. During that time my wife, who was working at Bullock's Department Store in Los Angeles, supported me. I sold a few short stories about the war, but they didn't bring in enough money to pay the light bill. I got a job as a newspaper reporter on the *Culver City Star,* but when the publisher who hired me on a veterans' program left, I was fired because I didn't have a car.

It was then that my wife suggested I go back to college and get my teaching credentials. Teaching paid only $2,800 *a year* to start in 1950. After twenty-seven years, I was at the top of the pay scale in Los Angeles at $20,000. I taught American history and English in junior high school for five years, and English, American literature, and world literature in high school for twenty-two years. After a heart attack, I retired on a pension of $850 a month. (In 2003, teachers start at about $30,000 a year.)

Before retiring, I studied photography at night school. I was fortunate to immediately sell photos to our local weekly newspaper and became its chief freelance photographer. I set up my own darkroom and studio and got by with what I earned plus my teacher's retirement. My three children had left home to strike out on their own. I hated to see them go because I loved them, but I couldn't interfere with their desires. I always regretted that I had never earned enough to help them financially. It seems that all of my adult life I worked two jobs just to keep my head above water.

My wife became very ill and spent three months in a convalescent hospital. She was always afraid to be alone, so I quit everything and was by her side every day and sometimes all night. She went into a coma. The day before she died, she opened her eyes and looked at me. I said, "Do you know who I am?" She said, "Yes, you're Joe, my husband." She again lapsed into a coma and died the next day, April 27, 2001, at 4:10 in the afternoon.

Since then I've sold my home for a good price, given each of my three children a one-third share from the profit, and gloried that at last I could give them something I'd never been able to give before.

According to my doctors, I might live another year or two. That doesn't bother me. I've never been afraid to die, and at eighty-eight, I've lived long enough.